The Rainbow Bridge
A Comparative Study of
Tagore and Sri Aurobindo

The Rainbow Bridge

A Comparative Study of Tagore and Sri Aurobindo

Goutam Ghosal

D.K. Printworld (P) Ltd.
New Delhi-110015

Cataloging in Publication Data — DK

[Courtesy: D.K. Agencies (P) Ltd. <docinfo@dkagencies.com>]

Ghosal, Goutam, 1953-

The rainbow bridge : a comparative study of Tagore and Sri Aurobindo / by Goutam Ghosal.

x, 235 p. 23 cm.

Includes bibliographical references (p.)

Includes index.

ISBN 8124604185

1. Tagore, Rabindranath, 1861-1941 — Criticism and interpretation. 2. Sri Aurobindo, 1872-1950. — Criticism and interpretation. I. Title.

DDC 891.441 409 22

ISBN 81-246-0418-5

First published in India in 2007

Published and printed by:

D.K. Printworld (P) Ltd.

Regd. Office: 'Sri Kunj', F-52, Bali Nagar

Ramesh Nagar Metro Station

New Delhi-110 015

Phones: (011) 2545-3975; 2546-6019; *Fax*: (011) 2546-5926

E-mail: dkprintworld@vsnl.net

Website: www.dkprintworld.com

I had hoped to build a rainbow bridge
Marrying the soil to the sky
And sow in this dancing planet midge
The moods of infinity.

— *A God's Labour,* Sri Aurobindo

Blessings have I won in this life of the Beautiful.

— Rabindranath Tagore

Preface

EDUCATED on an alien soil, Sri Aurobindo was back in India in 1893, in the crucial moments of resurgence. Tagore was then about to take up the mantle of "culture hero" from Bankim Chandra Chatterjee. And Vivekananda was going out to the West to announce the message of true India. Primarily poets, Tagore and Sri Aurobindo were never out of action. Contrary to the popular belief, Tagore worked hard with his own socio-political agendas under the guise of an "innocent" poet. The poet's glory dimmed the patriot.

Despite his questionable concept of nationalism preached in 1917, he did enough service to the nation and humanity through his mighty pen. He remains the soul of Bengali culture and of late many Indians from other provinces have been taking interest in him. His international fame is on the rise, thanks to the efforts of the translators, both from the West and the East.

Sri Aurobindo, never a public figure from 1910 to the day of his death in 1950, has been asserting his relevance to the present and the future since the beginning of the new millennium. It has now become obvious that together the two poets stand as the chief architects of a modern Indian tradition. This comparative study seeks to find the links between them, the cultural issues that bind them together. By and large, mine is an integral approach, an effort at interpreting their total achievement as poet-prophets of humanity. The book intends to shed light on the meaning of their contemporaneity.

7 Sevapalli, **Goutam Ghosal**
Santiniketan — 731235
West Bengal

Contents

1

Introduction

THE link between Tagore and Sri Aurobindo has been too insufficiently explored. One searches in vain for a "critical" comparative study of the two writers, the awesome two, who form the modern Indian tradition. Criticism is suspect. Even Goethe's suggestion — "Criticize we must, but on bended knees"[1] — remains unacceptable to the devotees of Tagore and Sri Aurobindo. But mere worship and critical neglect send a writer to the dusty shelves of a library. Not many have noticed that *The Life Divine* itself is a very critical text, which leaves the past scriptures behind by the pressure of progressive enlightenment. Such are also the leading texts of Tagore.

Rabindranath Tagore suffered long in the hands of his devotees, till Buddhadeva Bose and Sisirkumar Ghose rescued him and gave a new life to his works. Sri Aurobindo was fortunate, because his detractors kept criticizing him for the last five decades and a man called K.D. Sethna kept answering them, backed up by K.R.S. Iyengar, V.K. Gokak, Sisirkumar Ghose and a few others. Thanks to the hostile views on Sri Aurobindo, the researcher of the Supramental has now crept into the university canteens and tea-stalls! Similarly, Tagore continues to live his glorious life despite the revelations made

---

1. Sisirkumar Ghose, *Rabindranath Tagore*, New Delhi, Sahitya Akademi, 1986, see Preface, where Ghose has referred to Goethe's words to show an identical point of view.

by Ketaki Kusari Dyson.[2] Has not Sri Aurobindo told us that human beings are always mixed?[3] Those revelations do not degrade the finer qualities of Tagore or his very fine mystic poetry verging quite often on the spiritual plane.

Tagore would have laughed at the idea of being spiritually equated with the trekker of the Supermind and Sri Aurobindo would have mocked at the idea that there was just one great writer in the world called Sri Aurobindo. The point is: both are writers of superior status; both believe in inner victories; both are Indians and global at the same time; both are important for the future of India and humanity; the works of both are complementary for the most part. One lights up the status of the other. Realization colours their works. The degree and intensity of realization may not be the same. Unfortunately, Tagore wrote in Bengali, which helps only a particular race to feel the spiritual touch behind his aesthetics. In translation, the authentic experiential flavour is gone. Tagore has prepared a language for spiritual use. A mellow Bengali sensitivity, the grandeur of Sanskrit words and the aspiration of *Vaisnava Padavali* — all these three have contributed to the making of a language, which is now for the use of the Aurobindonians writing in Bengali. The success of Jyotirmala[4] is just a pointer to the fact.

Tagore was born in Calcutta, eleven years before Sri Aurobindo's birth, in 1861, when the nation was waking up in the heat of New Thinking. His family was well-off and cultured,

2. Ketaki Kusari Dyson, *Rabindranath O Victoria Okampor Sadhane,* Calcutta, Deys, 1997.
3. Sri Aurobindo, *Sri Aurobindo Birth Centenary Volume,* 23, Pondicherry, Sri Aurobindo Ashram, 1970, p. 561.
4. Original name Jyotirmoyee, who wrote poetry in Bengali under the guidance of Sri Aurobindo.

but luxury was not allowed to spoil him and the other children growing up with him under the supervision of servants. The school was a terror for the imaginative child and he could not move far with formal education. The cultural environment in the family was an immense help for young Rabindranath. There was that special company of Devendranath Tagore, his father, who took him to England in 1878 and kept the young poet with him for two years. Just a year later, Sri Aurobindo reached England and joined school to begin a bright academic career. The two heroes of the modern scene stayed close without knowing each other. Both were writing poetry from their childhood; both were bent on creating language; both were under the spell of the romantic poets who had just preceded them. The heat of nationalism touched Sri Aurobindo in England, possibly in the mid-1880s through the letters from his father. The heat increased in 1890 when news from India began flowing in the corridors of Cambridge, in its lusty lawns, which might have been temptation enough for a brilliant student. To the older poet, the heat had reached earlier.

Unlike Sri Aurobindo, Tagore was not an activist, but he was not at all innocuous in the eyes of the rulers. They detected quite early the camouflaged rebel trying to spread national education, through the ideas of an alternative school and through positive ventures at village reconstruction. In 1906, Tagore was known more as a poet than as a nationalist, although he was by then directly involved in *svadeshi.* Sri Aurobindo was simply known then as an "extremist" with an outstanding command over the English language. As the editor of *Bande Mataram,* he was bitingly aggressive, but he was always constructive with his views on the doctrine of boycott and passive resistance. He became quiet when he came out of jail in 1909. Talking then of the national awakening in Bengal he spoke of the lyrical spirit in Bengal very significantly and after that singled out Abanindranath Tagore as a great force in favour of nationalism.

> The lyric and the lyrical spirit, the spirit of simple, direct and poignant expression, of deep, passionate, straightforward emotion, of a frank and exalted enthusiasm, the dominant note of love and *bhakti,* of a mingled sweetness and strength, the potent intellect dominated by the self-illuminated heart, a mystical exaltation of feeling and spiritual insight expressing itself with a plain concreteness and practicality — this is the soul of Bengal. . . . In Bengal, again, the national spirit is seeking to satisfy itself in art and, for the first time since the decline of the Moguls, a new school of national art is developing itself, the school of which Abanindranath Tagore is the founder and master.[5]

Apart from offering a distinct hint at Rabindranath's genius, the passage also indicates Sri Aurobindo's approval of Abanindranath as a nationalist force working in collaboration with the activists. About a decade later, Rabindranath Tagore appears in *The Future Poetry* on sixteen different occasions. Here is a significant observation:

> Today much of the poetry of Tagore is the sign of such a *sadhana,* a long inheritance of an assured spiritual discovery and experience.[6]

Talking of the future of poetry, he remembers the Bengali lyricist repeatedly, finding in him signs of incantation and the promise of evolution in the lines drawn up by him in *The Future Poetry*. In the 1930s, Tagore appears again and again in his letters on poetry reflecting the controversies going on in Bengal then regarding Tagore's experiments.

---

5. Sri Aurobindo, *SABCL,* vol. 2, p. 39.
6. Sri Aurobindo, *SABCL,* vol. 9, p. 218.

Tagore met Sri Aurobindo twice, very humbly, recognizing in him the light unerringly. Sri Aurobindo's famous tribute needs to be interpreted properly. One seldom sees an interpretation added to that oft-quoted statement. Let us examine that remark again:

> Tagore has been a wayfarer towards the same goal as ours in his own way — that is the main thing, the exact stage of advance and putting of the steps are minor matters. His exact position as a poet or a prophet or anything else will be assigned by posterity and we need not be in haste to anticipate the final verdict.[7]

The statement contains quite a few subtle hints within a balanced structure. The beginning is a striking recognition and a caution to those who still believe Tagore should not be called a spiritual seeker or a *sadhak*. One easily feels the emphasis on the expression "that is the main thing." By the phrase "in his own way" Sri Aurobindo possibly meant his musical way, which is a powerful means of opening the psychic and inviting the higher sources to change the consciousness. The inward turn is enough achievement in a man's life; the rest is a matter of time and Grace of the Divine. Hence, he says, "Putting of the steps are minor matters." The last sentence is expressive of Sri Aurobindo's critical stance, which relies a lot on the future, on the judgement of posterity. He seems to have been unwilling to give his own verdict on the poet and the prophet.

For practical reasons, one suspects, Sri Aurobindo wished to leave the "final verdict" in the hands of the future. Tagore was his contemporary, a Bengali poet, immensely popular, and his school was also popular. Here, Sri Aurobindo was

---

7. Sri Aurobindo, *SABCL,* vol. 26, p. 346.

bound to curb his usual straightforwardness. And yet on another day, at another time, he spoke boldly in defence of Tagore's English *Gitanjali*:

> Tagore's *Gitanjali* is not in verse, but the place it has taken has some significance. For, the obstacles from the other side are that the English mind is apt to look on poetry by an Indian as a curiosity, something exotic (whether it really is or not, the suggestion will be there), and to stress the distance at which the English temperament stands from the Indian temperament. But Tagore's *Gitanjali* is most un-English, yet it overcame this obstacle.[8]

Time and again, Sri Aurobindo remembers the Bengali poet to indicate the change that will take place in the poetry of the future. Tagore, equally conscious, recognizes the achievement of the poet of *yoga*: "I thought he would light up the outside with his inner light."[9] Together, they began a new age of Indian poetry, Indian aesthetics and a new age of Indian spirituality, which refuses to ignore material life.

II

In constructing a new theory of poetry based on an old poetics, Sri Aurobindo specially refers to his favourite trio: Tagore, Whitman and Carpenter. The idea is to draw our notice to the new ways in poetry, which bear the memory of the great Sanskrit poets of ancient India. The trio should not be mistaken for some mere revivalists. For all of them seem to have been aware of the dynamic nature of the poetry of incantation or *mantra*. The stress on Tagore in *The Future Poetry* points to the

---

8. Sri Aurobindo, *SABCL*, vol. 9, p. 453.
9. Rabindranath Tagore, *Aurobindo Ghose*, written in Bengali, in 1928 just after his historic meeting with Sri Aurobindo in Pondicherry.

new theory, which Sri Aurobindo himself was trying to materialize in his own style. Sri Aurobindo observes:

> The poetry of Tagore owes its sudden and universal success to this advantage that he gives us more of this discovery and fusion for which the mind of our age is in quest than any other creative writer of the time. His work is a constant music of the overpassing of the borders, a chant-filled realm in which the subtle sounds and lights of the truth of the spirit give new meanings to the finer subtleties of life. The objection has been made that this poetry is too subtle and remote and goes away from the broad, near, present and vital actualities of existence. Yeats is considered by some a poet of the Celtic romance and nothing more, Tagore accused in his own country of an unsubstantial poetic philosophizing, a lack of actuality, reality of touch and force of vital insistence. But this is to mistake the work of this poetry and to mistake too in a great measure the sense of life, as it must reveal itself to the greatening mind of humanity now that it is growing in world-knowledge and towards self-knowledge.[10]

Tagore was a living example before Sri Aurobindo, who was then searching for the traces of mantric poetry in his contemporaries or near-contemporaries. The poetry as a rhythmic voice of inner life or the poetry of vision had virtually been too infrequent in the English poetry before the arrival of Whitman and Carpenter.

In Vedic Sanskrit, the word *kavi* meant the person who simply saw the inspired word and sang. He was not a logical analyser or scientific reasoner. He was neither a thinker nor a philosopher proper. He just saw and recorded his vision. Rhythm or music used to be born out of the inmost being of

---

10. Sri Aurobindo, *SABCL*, vol. 9, p. 229.

the poet or from the higher sources of inspiration. Vision is the keyword in Sri Aurobindo's theory of mantric poetry; vision was the essential poetic gift in the ancient seer-poets of India. The interference of intellect means the exit of vision. The prophet or the philosopher intellectualises; the true poet sees straight the living face of Truth.

> The inspired word comes, as said of the old Vedic seers, from the home of truth, *sadanād ṛtasya,* the high and native level of a superior self which holds the light of a reality that is hidden by the lesser truth of the normal sense and intelligence. It is rare, however, that it comes direct and unaltered, ready embodied and perfect and absolute . . .[11]

The perfect word is distorted quite often, because the intellectual mind interrupts the flow of the message, moulds it, and gives its own intellectual interpretation of the true message. Inspired poets like Tagore and Whitman have been deliberate in rejecting the excessive interference of the intellect. Instead, they indulged in the free play of the intuitive reason, the intuitive senses and the intuitive delight soul residing in them. Speaking for Tagore and Whitman, Sri Aurobindo was virtually speaking for himself. It was a distinct revolt against any kind of intellectual poetry. Tagore was important to Sri Aurobindo, because he indulged in finer passions, fancy, dream and imagination. All subjective poetry tends to turn inward and this inwardization opens up possibilities for the visional stuff. In the case of intellectual poetry, the brain remains overactive. The result is the birth of a poetry from the thinking mind, a poetry which is manufactured with great labour. Discouraging this practice, Sri Aurobindo takes us back to the ancient poets to clarify the essential nature and role of poetry.

11. Ibid., p. 279.

> To us poetry is a reveal of intellect and fancy, imagination a plaything and caterer for our amusement, our entertainer, the nautch-girl of the mind. But to the men of old the poet was a seer, a revealer of hidden truths, imagination no dancing courtesan but a priestess in God's house commissioned not to spin fictions but to image difficult and hidden truths; even the metaphor or simile in the Vedic style is used with a serious purpose and expected to convey a reality, not to suggest a pleasing artifice of thought.[12]

Tagore was the first Bengali poet to revive the true spirit of poetry with a deliberate memory of the Upanishads. He had an additional advantage: he was a spontaneous singer. It is this element in him that instantly relates him to the Sanskrit poets of the past. Sri Aurobindo's words shed illuminating light on his poetic or musical achievement. "A balanced harmony maintained by a system of subtle recurrences is the foundation of immortality in created things, and material movement is simply creative sound grown conscious of this secret of its own powers."[13] Even when Tagore has broken his Bengali rhythm in his English translations, something of a strange rhythmic voice is heard in the new creation.

> That gleaming look from the dark came upon me like a breeze that sends a shiver through the rippling water and sweeps away to the shadowy shore.[14]

Yet, it is impossible for a person without the knowledge of the Bengali language to feel the magical music of Tagore's lyrics in original. Sri Aurobindo might be thinking of the wonderful recreations included in *Gitanjali* (1912) and *Gardener*

12. Sri Aurobindo, *SABCL,* vol. 15, p. 5.
13. Sri Aurobindo, *SABCL,* vol. 9, p. 19.
14. Sisir Kumar Das (ed.), *The English Writings of Rabindranath Tagore,* vol. 1, New Delhi, Sahitya Akademi, 1994, p. 94.

(1913). The citation above shows that "unusual bringing together of words,"[15] which, according to Sri Aurobindo, is one characteristic of the poetry of incantation or *mantra*. As the original defied translation, Tagore wished to discover fresh lines of incantation in the English language. Even in his acquired tongue, Tagore could bring forward something from behind the mind or the vital emotion or the physical being, something which speaks of the cosmic self and its consciousness. Instances abound in his English writings, which may not seem Queen's English to many purists of the language.

> A flutter of flitting touch brushed me and vanished in a moment, like a torn flower petal blown in the breeze.[16]

Amidst judgements and statements on life, he discovers from time to time the secret vibrations of the soul, which go beyond all analysis. Such inspired selections are more frequent in his original Bengali poems.

III

Like Sri Aurobindo, Tagore wishes to see life as a whole. Every experience pushes us towards the Infinite through a natural process of evolution. One can hasten this process of evolution from nature to Supernature; the other may prefer a slow, leisurely walk. But, once the soul has become aware of the Divine, there is no going back to sleep again. Both of them dream of a new species on earth, although the present image of man shows little hope. They are infinitely optimistic because of their steady faith in the Divine. They know that the change of the individual is a condition for the change of the earth-consciousness. Society is the enlargement of the individual.

---

15. K.D. Sethna (ed.), *Overhead Poetry*, Pondicherry, Sri Aurobindo, International Centre of Education, 1972, p. 54.

16. Sisir Kumar Das, op. cit., p. 95.

Both have a strong aspiration for Beauty. Sri Aurobindo's *yoga* is a call for the Beauty of the Light to descend on earth. It does surround his life. Tagore has at least the power to materialize his dream of Beauty in his poetry. Nolini Kanto Gupta believes that the central motive in Tagore's poetry is an aspiration for Beauty.[17] He observes Beauty and expresses that Beauty beautifully. He culls Beauty from everywhere, — from Nature or from his inmost self — and creates an ideal Beauty. The sense expresses Beauty; the language expresses Beauty. Tagore is a magician of Beauty. The creation of Beauty is the inner law of his nature, his *svadharma.* The inner Tagore has appeared from the land of Beauty. "Knowledge and power have occupied a lower place in his consciousness," says Nolini Kanto Gupta, "They have remained there as the obedient servant of Beauty."[18] This sense of Beauty is the basic foundation of his concept of love, truth and goodness. His concept of nationalism is governed by his sense of Beauty. He does not wish to quarrel with the foreign rulers; he wishes to construct with the help of internal harmony. He has helped the descent of Beauty in the practical life of Bengal, which had long suffered from the lack of vitality, denial of life, poverty, frustration and a general state of chaos. Nolini Kanto Gupta's remarkable observation helps us understand the basic law of Tagore's nature. It is this sense of Beauty that integrates all the other aspects of Tagore's life and works.

Beauty is also a guiding force in Sri Aurobindo's life and works. There is the same equation of Beauty and love that we see in Tagore. Sri Aurobindo has harmonized with them the element of Knowledge and Power, austerity and the discipline

---

17. Nolini Kanto Gupta, *Rabindranath,* Kolkata, Sri Aurobindo Pathamandir, 1942, p. 2.

18. Ibid.

of *yoga*. Both are in love with the world, which is suffering in pain. They have two different ways to help her. One of their ways is identical: poetry. Tagore's poetry has a soothing effect. Sri Aurobindo's art is less attractive, but more active. If poetry can heal and fulfil, here is the poet, who has lived beyond the public gaze. The following lines from Sri Aurobindo will speak of the combined effect of Love, Knowledge and Beauty:

> Our hidden centres of celestial force
> Open like flowers to a heavenly atmosphere;
> Mind pauses thrilled with the supernal Ray,
> And even the transient body then can feel
>
> Ideal love and flawless happiness
> And laughter of the heart's sweetness and delight
> Freed from the rude and tragic hold of Time,
> And beauty and the rhythmic feet of the hours.[19]

Tagore has his own sweet ways to describe things of beauty. He is close to us and speaks of familiar things, which have escaped our notice:

> I filled my tray whatever I had, and gave it to you. What shall I bring to your feet tomorrow, I wonder. I am like the tree that, at the end of the flowering summer, gazes at the sky with its lifted branches bare of their blossoms.[20]

Tagore transfers the feminine element of his mother tongue into his acquired language. His language lacks the masculine force of Sri Aurobindo's Poetry. But who can deny the new charm in Tagore's poetry? Both the poets seek to express the totality of life, the integral vision of life. Less logical than Sri Aurobindo in his prose, Tagore has a roundabout

---

19. Sri Aurobindo, *Savitri*: *A Legend and a Symbol*, Pondicherry, Sri Aurobindo Ashram, 1950, p. 252.

20. Sisir Kumar Das, op. cit., p. 204.

way of logicizing with the help of superior poetry. By and large, it is an intuitive logic specially discovered in the Bengali language.

When we go through Tagore's early poetry, we do not fail to see his restless yearning for a romantic world of beauty. The yearning matured around 1912 and then it became less frequent in his poetry. Although his prose retained the yearning, his later poetry moved in various directions and changed its complexion frequently. From the middle of 1870s till 1912, we see him struggling to search for the *Essence* behind the common flavours of life. The immature poetry of his teens speaks of a Vaisnava poet of the new age. Sri Aurobindo saw him in the right light before leaving for Pondicherry in 1910.

> One of the remarkable peculiarities of Rabindra Babu's genius is the happiness and originality with which he has absorbed the whole spirit of Vaisnava poetry and turned it into something essentially the same and yet new and modern. He has given the old sweet spirit of emotional and passionate religion an expression of more delicate and complex richness voiceful of shutter and more penetratingly spiritual shades of feeling than the deep-hearted but simple early age of Bengal could know. The old Vaisnava *bhāva* — there is no English word for it — was easily seizable, broad and strong. The *bhāva* of these poems is not translatable in any other language than the poet has used. . . .[21]

This spirit of Vaisnavism fused curiously with his quest for a natural ecstasy. He would like to take delight in the things that came to him naturally. He felt the eternal around him in the natural objects. We see in him a strange yearning for a half-identified beloved in his early poetry. We find it in the poem entitled *Upahar*. Woman or someone else, one cannot be

---

21. Sri Aurobindo, *SABCL*, vol. 3, pp. 430-31.

certain:

> I have forgot when you came close to my heart
> one day in my childhood
> Fond and shadowy, you laughed once perhaps
> opening your eyes like the dusk. . . .[22]

In *Probhat Utsab* (Festival of the Dawn) another early poem, Tagore projects his cosmic awareness. This might have been the influence of Walt Whitman. However, the realisation seems genuine and his language too speaks of his own awareness.

> Who knows how
> my soul has opened up today,
> all the universe is gathered
> in the self.
>
> All men under the sun
> have found their place over there,
> they laugh in intimate embrace.[23]

In *Ananta Jibon* (Infinite Life), the poet expresses his awareness of the Divine.

> At the centre of this Universe
> there is an ocean,
> its water is silent.
> From all its sides
> streams come incessantly to merge in it.[24]

The young poet lacks in concrete images, but his growing perception is unmistakable. Sometimes, there creeps in the typical mysticism of Tagore in immature verse. But then, even in his immaturity, the effort to discover an original voice is

---

22. Rabindranath Tagore, *Rabindra-Rachanaboli* (Sulabh Sanskaran), Kolkata: Visva-Bharati, 2002, p. 38.
23. Ibid., p. 55.
24. Ibid., p. 57.

much too obvious. Let us attempt a translation from *Punormilon* (*Reunion*).

> The swan floats on
> throughout the day
> from shore to another shore,
> it washes its wings clean
> from time to time.
> On the east, stands the old banyan tree
> with thick leaves on its top
> It stands with its vast awful shadows.[25]

This is mysticism in the nursery class. This manner grows and deepens throughout the 1880s and towards the close of the century it shapes itself out in an original mystic style. The strong attachment for the earth is visible even in his early poetry, which is quite in harmony with the mystic sense. The mature mystic manner is to be found in *Sonar Tori, Chitra, Nabedyo, Gitimalya, Gitanjali* and the other poems of the middle period.

---

25. Ibid., p. 62.

2

Formative Influences

RELIGION meant very little to Sri Aurobindo in his teens. It meant a lot to Tagore; he was steeped in the Brahmo cult since his childhood. However, religion and spirituality were not the only tunes that rang in the Tagore house at Jorasanko. The Tagores were fond of poetry, painting, theatre, music and almost all the arts under the sun. Young Rabindranath hated confinement. His mind pined for far away things. Sri Aurobindo would have called him a typical "mystic" child fond of exploring twilit lanes, wishing for the paths, but not for the goal in a one-pointed labour. He talked of the goal and the pain of eternal separation, but the variety of the Divine on the material plane distracted his attention quite often.

The sweet rhythmic verse of *Vaisnava Padavali* cast a spell on him early in his life. The aesthete was not able to define why he was drawn to those mysterious verses. He was a Nature-mystic by birth. He was curious about the hidden Supremo, who reflected Himself in all His creations. He wished to imagine Him in many ways. He imagined Him in terms of aesthetics, the aesthetics reaching him through the English Romantics like Shelley and Keats, sometimes directly, and often through a poet named Biharilal Chakraborty who was tremendously popular during Tagore's boyhood and early youth. The close association with Devendranath, his father, helped him reach the Upanishads and other scriptures of the world. Besides, there were the great musicians around him, the great singers from different fields of music. They took away his heart.

Outside the great house of Jorasanko, the streets were filled with the cry for freedom. Inside, the great Tagores were stirred by that cry. The thinking mind of Tagore was also developing by the touch of the great intellectuals who thronged the corridors of *Thakurbari.* Then there was that proverbial self-training. Niharranjan Ray draws our attention to "his unceasing and life-long attempt to weave into the pattern of his being whatever was creative in thought, imagination and vision of India's past, from the days of the Veda and Upanishads right up to his own. Formally and spiritually, he aimed at an interpenetration and complete identification of his individual personality with the personality of India as he saw and understood it."[1]

Sri Aurobindo was divorced from his native soil at the age of seven, when he was sent to England for a formal education. Initially, his father wished him to grow up as an anglicized intellectual. From his seventh to twenty-first year, he was in England learning all the finer elements of European culture and acquiring glamorous degrees. It was towards the close of his stay in England that he began to feel strongly for his motherland. The feeling deepened the moment he returned to his native soil. He learnt Sanskrit quickly, took a close look at the contemporary situation, and transformed himself into a true Indian, who could see the past and the present of the country with a swift synthetic glance. He could not ignore anybody speaking deprecatingly of India. Here was a man of extreme temperament, sometimes angry and often totally dispassionate. When the heat of New Nationalism mellowed

1. Rabindranath Tagore, (1861-1961), *A Centenary Volume,* Sahitya Akademi, New Delhi, 1961, p. 224.

and he was released from jail in 1909, his voice was that of a new man. The anger was gone. His writings mirrored the change of his consciousness. In 1910, he reached Pondicherry to play a new role. From 1914 onwards, the author could synthesize the best of Europe and Asia. The global tradition behind him became quite prominent in the *Arya* period (1914-21). With the new power of expression, there appeared a global prose indicating his assimilation of the past. He was not reading much in Pondicherry; he was just writing without secretarial assistance. It was a memory of his past acquaintance with the ancient Indian and European literature. Reading became very casual for the poet of *yoga* (1910-50). The memory of past readings is clear in the comparative modes:

> Therefore we see that the reason in its growth either does away with the distinct spiritual tendency for a time, as in ancient Greece, or accepts it but spins out around its first data and activities a vast web of the workings of the intelligence, so that, as in India, the early mystic seer is replaced by the philosopher-mystic, the religious thinker and even the philosopher pure and simple.[2]

It is curious that Sri Aurobindo's prose had not reflected such a wonderful synthetic mind in Calcutta and Baroda. For Tagore, the assimilation of thoughts was immediately known, just after the work of assimilation. But the proper Western "historical sense" of Sri Aurobindo was projected only in his Pondicherry prose. Of course, he had written fine comparative criticism in Baroda, in pieces like *Hindu Drama* and in the notes on the great Indian epics. But then, it became a more solid and a more frequent stylistic device in Pondicherry (1914-50). Was it a case of improvement in Sri Aurobindo's expression? Or was it just because he did not have his subject proper in

2. Sri Aurobindo, *SABCL*, vol. 15, p. 177.

Baroda and Calcutta? It is difficult to guess. Unlike Tagore, Sri Aurobindo does not give us any specific indication about the influences on him.

To deny the spiritual quest of Tagore is a serious critical blindness. Of late, this blindness has become infectious in Bengal because of Ketaki Kusari Dyson's discovery of the passionate nature of Tagore at the age of sixty-three.[3] This is not a new discovery, as his poetry was never secretive and this does not degrade the spiritual side of Tagore, the man. If "spiritual" means everything equal to Sri Aurobindo, Sri Ramakrishna and Sri Chaitanya, then of course it is another matter. But, it would be a serious critical mistake to underestimate the enlightened soul-status of Tagore. Both Tagore and Sri Aurobindo woke up to the mystic smell quite early in life. For Sri Aurobindo, it was not quite obvious because religion was not his cup of tea in England. Yet we should not overlook the quality of endurance and equanimity in the schoolboy, who had no complaints against Dr. Krishnadhan Ghose, a negligent father, who forgot quite often to send in the money required by his sons in England. Also, Sri Aurobindo's early poetry written in England speaks of his early approaches to Nature and the Divine:

Sweet is the night, sweet and cool
As to parched lips a running pool;
Sweet when the flowers have fallen asleep
And only moonlit rivulets creep
Like glow-worms in the dim and whispering wood
To commune with the quiet heart and solitude.[4]

---

3. Ketaki Kusari Dyson, *In Your Blossoming Flower-Garden: Rabindranath Tagore and Victoria Ocampo*, New Delhi, Sahitya Akademi, p. 271.

4. Sri Aurobindo, *SABCL*, vol. 5 (Collected Poems), p. 1.

In *Songs to Myrtilla,* he can already listen to the "footsteps of invisible things" and see the night "leaning on a luminous cloud." The secret voice of the Divine can be heard when Nature smiles and love is awake with its mysterious signals through a mystic rose. The vision of Beauty at the end of *Songs to Myrtilla* is not just Keatsian; it is a prescience of a great discovery to be made by the poet of *Savitri.*

Tagore, too, seems to have been an early riser. Time and again he tells us that his is not a one-pointed search. He wishes to be lost in the Many with a constant memory of the One. He speaks about his many-branching desires. And yet who could deny his early approaches to the Divine?

> When I was eighteen, a sudden spring breeze of religious experience came to my life for the first time and passed away leaving in my memory a direct message of spiritual reality. One day while I stood watching at early dawn the sun sending out its rays from behind the trees, I suddenly felt as if some ancient mist had in a moment lifted from my sight, and the morning light in the face of the world revealed an inner radiance of joy. The invisible screen of the commonplace was removed from all things and men, and their ultimate significance was intensified in my mind; and this is the definition of beauty. That which was memorable in this experience was its human message, the sudden expansion of my consciousness in the super-personal world of man. The poem I wrote on the first day of my surprise was called *The Awakening of the Waterfall.* The waterfall, whose spirit lay dormant in its ice-bound isolation, was touched by the sun and, bursting in a cataract of freedom, it found its finality in an unending sacrifice, in a continual union with the sea. After four days the vision passed away, and the lid

> hung down upon my inner sight. In the dark, the world once again put on its disguise of obscurity.[5]

This is a mystical experience presented in terms of aesthetics, unlike the more direct spiritual experiences of Sri Aurobindo in Alipur jail, which he records in very clear terms. Tagore was aware of his mysterious presentation of mystical experience. He was fond of it; he indulged in it throughout his life. The Bengali language as we have received it from Tagore is a feminine language and is ideally suited to the mystic mind, who deals with the borderline romance. The expression of the Truth in its essential nakedness was not the aim of Tagore. That feature makes Sri Aurobindo a less attractive poet for the general audience because only a few in the present humanity can go close to those experiences.

Tagore is a wonderful preparation for understanding the absolutely one-pointed poetry of Sri Aurobindo. The Godward emotion was a reality in Tagore's personal life and works. It remained throughout with him, sometimes very intensely and sometimes in a subterranean manner. That gave a delicate charm and beauty to his borderline experiences, as in *Gitanjali* and *The Post Office,* and helped him develop his integral philosophy, which links him up with Sri Aurobindo. The early riser never went to sleep again. He attempted to assort aesthetics with inner realizations. There is no doubt about his realizations of the *more*:

> I frankly say that I cannot satisfactorily answer questions about the problem of evil, or about what happens after death. And yet I am sure that there have come moments when my

---

5. Sisirkumar Ghose (ed.), *Tagore For You,* Visva-Bharati, Calcutta, 1984, p. 6.

> soul has touched the infinite and has become intensely conscious of it through the illumination of joy.[6]

Sisirkumar Ghose has spoken of this queer assortment of aesthetics and spirituality in Tagore and has drawn our notice to his effort at integral realization. Ghose was a staunch Aurobindonian and as such it was easy for him to understand Tagore's effort in the true light:

> Tagore's life and works were, then, not merely an aesthete's adventure, dreaming of the surplus and the far away; they also involve characteristic enlarging moral choices in terms of an integrated or harmonious living. The founding of a school at Santiniketan (1901), later to be a university, was part of the education in fullness. Beginning with his own unhappy memory of school, which he described as a blend of hospital and gaol, he concentrated on children and emphasized creativity, the need for atmosphere and natural surroundings. The aim was neither ascetic nor revivalistic but integrative.[7]

Both the poets were drawn to Nature and God in their teens, but both were interested in experiencing life. They refused to reject life. All the tastes of life were welcome. Both were thinking of this earth, the ways to beautify or transform it. The labour began early in their lives. They dreamt. Here is young Aurobindo dreaming of man's future:

> The old shall perish; it shall pass away,
> Expunged, annihilated, blotted out;
> And all the iron bands that ring about
> Man's wide expansion shall at last give way.[8]

---

6. Ibid., pp. 49-50.

7. Ibid., p. 15.

8. Sri Aurobindo, *SABCL*, vol. 5, p. 61.

While Sri Aurobindo was a lonely traveller, Tagore was throughout in the company of men and women. He inherited the principles of the Upanishads from his father and could see his inside and the outer worlds simultaneously and never lost sight of the bridge between the two. He possibly learnt this lesson from his father at a very early age. Tagore's early poetry will testify to this. Like Sri Aurobindo, Tagore realized the value of his country quite early in his life. As a poet, he touched his native tradition earlier than Sri Aurobindo. It was just great luck to have such fantastic people around in the nineteenth-century Bengal. And the greatest luck was his father's company!

Both the poets were born romantics and naturally they were drawn to poets like Keats, Shelley and Tennyson. For Sri Aurobindo, the schoolboy, it was just the European "historical sense." For Tagore, it was "global" romanticism, a queer blend of Shelley, *Vaisnava Padavali* and Biharilal Chakraborty. Even in his teens, Tagore felt a cry within himself to grab something higher than him, to get out of the bondage of the desires pulling him downwards. Nature was the key tune. He felt a keen intimacy with Nature. In fact, he felt it keener than Wordsworth. He felt that he was part of the plants and shrubs, the streams, the come-and-go of winds, the constellations, the numerous animals and birds. The outer made a stir inside. It was cosmic consciousness, which was more Aurobindonian than Wordsworthian. Young Aurobindo could feel in another language the same vibrations in Nature. There were just memories of Keats and Tennyson and Wordsworth, but a new voice was clear from the very beginning. He claimed his originality very early in his life:

> Mine is not Byron's lightning spear,
> Nor Wordsworth's lucid strain

Nor Shelley's lyric pain,
Nor Keats', the poet without peer.
I by the Indian waters vast
Did glimpse the magic of the past. . . .[9]

But, Sri Aurobindo was a confused Indian at school, although, I suspect, a strong sense of separation was there throughout his stay in England. *Love in Sorrow* confirms that he was homesick to a degree. The subjectivism of the following lines authenticates his early effort at writing original lyrics:

For there was none who loved me, no, not one.
  Alas! what was there that a man should love?

For I was misery's last and frailest son
  And even my mother bade me homeless rove.[10]

Bad poetry or good poetry — that is not our point here. It confirms that Sri Aurobindo was not imitating Keats or Tennyson. He was searching for his own idiom in his teens, thinking aloud his own problems, just as Tagore did as a boy-poet. In his twenties, Sri Aurobindo could re-create Wordsworth in a new poetic idiom:

A golden evening, when the thoughtful sun
Rejects its usual pomp in going, trees
That bend down to their green companion
And fruitful mother, vaguely whispering, — these
And a wide silent sea. Such hour is nearest God, —
Like rich old age when the long ways have all been trod.[11]

Tagore and Sri Aurobindo were Nature-mystics even from their days of apprenticeship, when they were learning to perfect their art. Unlike Tagore, Sri Aurobindo was obsessed

---

9. Sri Aurobindo, *SABCL*, vol. 5, p. 8.

10. Ibid., p. 22.

11. Ibid., p. 46.

by the "rose." That image would grow into a large metaphor in his later poetry, in *Savitri* in particular. The "sea" is another image that grows and deepens in his later poetry.

Tagore was passionately attached to Nature. The attachment lasted throughout. He wished to see everything, every aspect of it, eagerly, as if he would not get another chance to observe its queer mysteries, as if this life was given to him to discover all the forms of Nature. He remembered the misty days of his childhood with great fondness, when he could just see a pond and a mysterious banyan tree by it with its long dense branches. It was real, and the early prose and poetry reflected his own passion for discovering the language. "It wasn't enriched, but it was mine,"[12] Tagore said about his *Sandhya Sangeet* (*Evening Songs*) indicating his claim for originality. The next year, in 1883, *Prabhat Sangeet* (*Morning Songs*) came out showing the prescience of the mature life-sense of Tagore, the life-sense that speaks of the presence of the Infinite in the finite, the presence of the whole in the part. It is that cosmic awareness, which we also see in Sri Aurobindo's poetry written during his twenties. Let us see how Tagore expresses his awareness of this mystery behind every object of Nature:

> In every nook and corner,
> in the scattered bushes and plants
> what wonder was lurking! and what awe!
> The birds sat on the branches
> and sang the same tune
> throughout the day
> the hush around
> made my heart throb,

12. *Rabindra Rachanabali* (Works of Tagore in Bengali), Kolkata, West Bengal Government, 1980, vol. 1, p. 4, from the Preface to *Sandhya Sangeet* (*Evening Songs*).

a warm wind kissed my body
bringing in strange things.[13]

It was also a kind of invitation of the *more* in the true spiritual sense. Tagore was unwilling to risk a one-pointed adventure. Instead, he began seeing and feeling this call of the *more* from the viewpoint of aesthetics. He chose to move on the shadowy borderline of aesthetics and spirituality:

My heart wishes
to go up into the sky
and live like the stars,
wishes to bloom
in its own joy
like flowers gazing at the sky,
wishes to go up in the sky
at dead of night
to look around,
wishes to lose its way
among the stars
and sing unmindfully.[14]

This queer blend of aesthetics and spirituality is more prominent in *The Flute* (*Kori O Komal*), which is another sign of the young Tagore's success in re-creating the mood of *Vaisnava Padavali* for the modern age. The note of yearning for the Lord is too serious here; it comes out authentically through the aesthetic medium:

O, listen to the flute,
who plays it?
the fragrance of the garland
merges into the tune of the flute . . .

---

13. Ibid., p. 77, translated by the author.
14. Ibid., p. 101, translated by the author.

I hear the musical sounds of Yamuna,
My soul sobs. . . .[15]

Sri Aurobindo's poetry, with its quest for originality all the time, matured speedily after 1895. As Tagore was preparing for *Sonar Tori* (*The Golden Boat,* 1894) and *Naivedya* (*Sacred Offerings,* 1901) on the verge of his fortieth year, Sri Aurobindo was preparing to greet his thirties with his mature poetry of cosmic awareness. There was not much of tradition behind Sri Aurobindo's mature poetry, except for the memories of Whitman and the Upanishads here and there. He was possibly attempting to see how romanticism could be channellized in a one-pointed direction. He was spontaneously seeking a new form to record his spiritual experiences. By then, the Divine became an obsessive quest for him. The fiery prose and the satirical editorials written in the early *Bande Mataram* (1906-07) period conceal this obsessive quest, which was going on in a subterranean manner.

The quest had begun in Baroda in the late 1890s and it deepened behind the public gaze and came to the surface in the post-jail prose and poetry (1909 onwards). On the contrary, the multi-dimensional poetry of Tagore was close to the human consciousness and the frequent "God-touch" in that poetry made Tagore very popular. Sri Aurobindo was less attractive even in the pre-Pondicherry days, simply because he chose God whole-heartedly as the only subject of his poetry. Except for some love poems written very early in his career, some mythical and philosophical poems and a few tributary lyrics, Sri Aurobindo could do nothing without the Divine. He was technically sound in those formative years — in Baroda and Calcutta — and he was soon able to master a very economical

15. Ibid., pp. 243-44.

style with little signs of any influence on him:

> My soul arose at dawn and, listening, heard
> One voice abroad, a solitary bird,
> A song not master of its note, a cry
> That persevered into eternity.[16]

Such were the two poets in their formative years. Both of them mastered prose in their early life, as if they were two born lords of language. One wrote in Bengali; the other in English. Tagore's *Torn Letters* or *Chhinna Patra* bear testimony to his early mastery of Bengali prose. Most of these letters were written to Indira Devi, his niece, from 1887 to 1895. This prose is simpler than Bankim Chandra's descriptive prose, but more attractive because its rhythm is close to the usual speech rhythm of the Bengali language.

> By this time the sun sets; the gold tint in the sky vanishes. In the dark, everything around becomes clear. Later, on seeing the faint shadow by me I come to know that the thin moon is up with its meagre light. You can't trust your eyes when you see the pale light over the pale sand. It is not a matter of guess where the sand and the water and the sky and the earth lie.[17]

I refer to this letter just to show how casually Tagore could write masterfully in his twenties. He created this language. It had not existed before him. The usual letter in Bengali in the pre-Tagore era had read like the language of metaphysics! *Europe Prabasir Patra* (*Letters of a Sojourner in Europe,* 1881) had been less interesting, but certainly as mature as the *Chhinna Patra.* Sri Aurobindo mastered the English language at about the age of eighteen. The document lies in a Dialogue entitled

16. Sri Aurobindo, *SABCL,* vol. 5, p. 41.
17. Rabindranath Tagore, *Chhinna Patra,* Kolkata, Visva-Bharati Granthan Bibhag 1912, p. 33.

The Harmony of Virtue (1890-92). He could not round off his arguments, probably because he lost interest by the middle of the piece. The language and the weight of thought behind it are just incredible as it came from the hands of a teenager:

> Look at the stars, the brain of heaven as Meredith calls them. How they march tossing on high their golden censers to perfume night with the frankincense of beauty! They are a host of winged insects crawling on the blue papyrus of heaven, a swarm of golden gnats, a cloud of burning dust, a wonderful effect of sparkling atoms caught and perpetuated by the instantaneous pencil of Nature. And yet they are none of all these, but a vast and interdependent economy of worlds. Those burning globes as they roll in silent orbits through the infinite inane, are separated by an eternity of space. They are individual and alone but from each to each thrill influences unfathomed and unconscious, marvellous magnetisms, curious repulsions that check like adverse gales or propel like wind in bellying canvas, and bind these solitary splendours into one supernal harmony of worlds.[18]

This prose could be a dream piece for any mature author. He wrote it possibly before he was eighteen. It might be that he reached the limit of his experience and left it incomplete. While he acknowledges the memory of Plato's *Republic and Symposium,* there are traces of the Wildean rhetoric here and there. Wilde's *The Decay of Lying* came out in 1889 and *The Critic as Artist* was published in 1890. Sri Aurobindo's immediate inspiration might have come from those two Dialogues of Wilde. Not that he liked the world-view of the famous Irishman. But he would enjoy his wit very much as his brother Manmohan, who was close to Wilde, would very often talk to young Aurobindo about him.

18. Sri Aurobindo, *SABCL,* vol. 3, p. 18.

3

Nationalism and Postnationalism

TAGORE'S book *Nationalism* was published by Macmillan, New York, in 1917. It attacked the Western ideas of nationalism directly and created a lot of controversy. In the *Notes to The English Writings of Rabindranath Tagore,* we find the following observation:

> Tagore's forthright denunciation of nationalism provoked violent attacks in the American press and severe criticism by the Japanese intellectuals. This work made him unpopular not only in America and Japan, but also in India where nationalism had already entered a new phase of growth. Tagore wrote his first political novel *Ghare Baire* (1916) — its English translation by Surendranath Tagore was published three years later — in which he criticized the Swadeshi movement very strongly. "His lectures on Nationalism", writes Kripalini, "were "ill-timed."[1]

It was ill timed, because India then badly needed to establish her own identity. Only a decade before, Sri Aurobindo, Bepin Pal and Tilak had preached and practised their gospel of New Nationalism. The time was not ripe in 1917 to preach the value of one world. The poet and the humanist blinded the politician. Yet here and there, in these essays, there are moments when Tagore, with his awareness of India's glorious past, comes close to Sri Aurobindo, the defender of Indian culture:

1. Sisir Kumar Das (ed.), *The English Writings of Rabindranath Tagore,* vol. II, New Delhi 2001, p. 771.

> Her mission has been that of a hostess who has to provide proper accommodation for numerous guests, whose habits and requirements are different from one another. This gives rise to infinite complexities whose solution depends not merely upon tactfulness but upon sympathy and true realization of the unity of man. Towards this realization have worked, from the early time of the Upanishads up to the present moment, a series of great spiritual leaders, whose one object has been to set at naught all differences of man by the overflow of our consciousness of God. In fact, our history has not been of the rise and fall of kingdoms, of fights for political supremacy. In our country records of these days have been despised and forgotten, for they in no way represent the true history of our people. Our history is that of our social life and attainment of spiritual ideals.[2]

The structure and the tone of the passage are in line with Sri Aurobindo's refutation and defence in *The Foundations of Indian Culture* (1918-21). Let us listen to Sri Aurobindo:

> The spirit and ideals of our civilization need no defence for in their best parts and in their essence they were of eternal value. India's internal and individual seeking of them was earnest, powerful, effective. But the application in the collective life of society was subjected to serious reserves. Never sufficiently bold and thoroughgoing it became more and more limited and halting when the life-force declined in her peoples. This defect, this gulf between ideal and collective practice, has pursued all human living and was not peculiar to India; but the dissonance became especially marked with the lapse of time and it put at last on our society a growing stamp of weakness and failure. There was a large effort in the beginning at some kind of synthesis between

2. Ibid., p. 420 (essay on Nationalism).

> the inner ideal and the outer life, but a static regulation of society was its later end. An underlying principle of spiritual idealism, an elusive unity and fixed helpful forms of mutuality remained always there, but also an increasing element of strict bondage and minute division and fissiparous complexity in the social mass.[3]

The two passages speak of the unbiased attitude of the interpreters, who are virtually exhibiting their sense of the native tradition. About a decade earlier, when Sri Aurobindo was proclaiming an aggressive nationalism in the editorials of *Bande Mataram*, he was quite logical and constructive. His nationalism was never extremism; it was a wrong label given to a very logical movement. From 1906 to 1909, in the journals entitled *Bande Mataram* and *Karmayogin*, he was carrying on an intellectual battle to codify the principles of New Nationalism. For him, as also for Tilak and Bepin Chandra Pal, the country was primary; the freedom of India was primary. The idiom of the activists was bold, but logic was never missing in that rhetoric. For everything there is a season. The hour demanded assertive gestures. Those leaders were not interested in preaching sophisticated humanism. They had a vision before them. India is not just a piece of land, but also a living image of the Mother or Mahashakti. Sandip in Tagore's *Ghare Baire* (1916) might have misused the ideal. But it was true for many Indians. What was the gospel of New Nationalism? How was Sri Aurobindo trying to visualize the ideal? The following passage will give a clear idea:

> So with India rests the future of the world. Whenever she is aroused from her sleep, she gives forth some wonderful shining ray of light to the world, which is enough to

3. Sri Aurobindo, *SABCL*, vol. 14, *The Foundations of Indian Culture*, pp. 36-37.

> illuminate the nations. Others live for centuries on what is to her the thought of a moment. God gave to her the book of Ancient Wisdom and bade her keep it seated in her heart, until the time should come for it to be opened. Sometimes a page or a chapter is revealed, sometimes only a single sentence. Such sentences have been the inspiration of ages and fed humanity for many hundreds of years. So too when India sleeps, materialism grows apace and the light is covered up in darkness. But when materialism thinks herself about to triumph, lo and behold! a light rushes out from the East and where is materialism? Returned to her native night.[4]

Sri Aurobindo had a firm conviction that the nation was developing swiftly in the early years of the twentieth century. Like Tagore, he was aware of the Indian heritage, the special features of the Indian heritage and the special features of a great country. By then, he was also certain of the evolutionary principles of life, which India had known well since the dawn of civilization. Later in 1917, Tagore remembers this India of the old days: ". . . the India devoid of all politics, the India of no nations, whose one ambition has been to know this world as of a soul, to live here every moment of her life in the meek spirit of adoration, in the glad consciousness of an eternal and personal relationship with it."[5]

Sri Aurobindo had known this quite well in 1909 and had attempted boldly to remind the people of India of this great heritage. But, certainly he seems to have been more specific than Tagore, more specific in the details relating to India's glorious past. Just an example will show his advanced vision:

---

4. Sri Aurobindo, *SABCL*, vol. 1, *Bande Mataram*, p. 71.
5. *The English Writings of Rabindranath Tagore,* vol. 2, p. 420, essay on *Nationalism*.

> One of the oldest races and greatest civilizations on this earth, the most indomitable in vitality, the most fecund in greatness, the deepest in life, the most wonderful in potentiality, after taking into itself numerous sources of strength from foreign strains of blood and other types of human civilization, is now seeking to lift itself for good into an organized national unity.[6]

While Tagore evades the question of eternal religion, in favour of what he calls "the truth of the human soul" (see essay on *Nationalism*), Sri Aurobindo comes out with a bolder voice in favour of a universal spirituality, which alone can change the consciousness of man. This call for a universal religion was part and parcel of New Nationalism, a thing synonymous with the voice of God. It was not the voice of a fanatic. The idea of a synthesis of multiple principles is obvious in the following passage:

> We do not believe that by multiplying new sects limited within the narrower and inferior ideas of religion imported from the West or by creating organizations for the perpetuation of the mere dress and body of Hinduism we can recover our spiritual health, energy and greatness. The world moves through an indispensable interregnum of free thought and materialism to a new synthesis of religious thought and experience, a new religious world-life free from intolerance, yet full of faith and fervour, accepting all forms of religion because it has an unshakable faith in the One. The religion which embraces Science and faith, Theism, Christianity, Muhammadism and Buddhism and yet is none of these, is that to which the World-Spirit moves.[7]

The passage reflects a prophecy or prescience of a synthesis of religions. It shows that Sri Aurobindo was not a fanatic

6. Sri Aurobindo, *SABCL*, vol. II, *Karmayogin*, p. 16.
7. Ibid., pp. 18-19.

during the days of his activism. This evolving spirit of universal spirituality, which is the basis of Sri Aurobindo's philosophy, is also the basis of Tagore's gospel of Nationalism. Unfortunately, Tagore did not take into consideration this essence of New Nationalism, when he attacked Nationalism at a wrong time, thinking wrongly that the nationalist movement in the then India was against the cause of humanity.[8]

Again, Tagore comes closer to Sri Aurobindo in *Creative Unity,* where he recognizes the value of both the Eastern spirituality and the Western materialism in the making of new ideal of living, which would be more complete and definitive, more synthetic and integral. Sri Aurobindo, the nationalist, speaks precisely about that in Calcutta. Tagore echoes the idea:

> The man from the East, with his faith in the eternal, who in his soul had met the touch of the Supreme Person — did he never come to you in the West and speak to you of the Kingdom of Heaven? Did he not unite the East and the West in truth, in the unity of one spiritual bond between all children of the immortal, in the realization of one great personality in all human persons? Yes, the East did once meet the West profoundly in the growth of her life. Such union became possible, because the East came to the West with the ideal that is creative, and not with the passion that destroys moral bonds. The mystic consciousness of the Infinite, which she brought with her, was greatly needed by the man of the West to give him his balance.[9]

The passage confirms the link between the two nationalists. Spirit has to be fused with Matter. Both Tagore and Sri Aurobindo are in love with this world and somehow they are

---

8. *The English Writings of Rabindranath Tagore,* vol. II, p. 458.
9. Ibid., pp. 536-37.

both thinking of a better future, where Spirit and Matter will live like a harmonious husband and wife. And yet, when we come to the point of nationalism in the first two decades of the twentieth century, Tagore's fear of it seems a bit awkward. Not that he could not see the country as Mother at any stage, but around 1917 he lost the vision of the country as Mahashakti. Sri Aurobindo, least affected by garlands and abuses, was never hesitant about an aggressive nationalism even as a Lover of Humanity. His love of India was perfectly harmonized with his love for man.

Contradiction is no sin, especially in a great poet. Tagore who wrote the book *Nationalism* in 1917 seems to have been disgusted with the world. The same person had inspired the nationalists in the last half of the nineteenth century, and more powerfully around 1905, when Sri Aurobindo had been preparing to give a new impetus to the nationalist movement, by shifting his focus from Baroda to Calcutta. Poems like *Prachin Bharat* (1897), *Bharat Lakshmi* (1898), *Bharat Tirtha* (1910) shows Tagore's cultural link with the mainstream nationalists. Like Sri Aurobindo, Tagore was keenly aware of the sacredness of his motherland:

> Awake, my mind,
> in this holy place of pilgrimage
> on the shore of vast humanity
> that is India.[10]
>
> — 1910

There was more direct inspiration for the nationalists:

> We, thousands, have strung together,
> we, thousands, have submitted ourselves
> to one single cause

10. Sisirkumar Ghose (ed.), *Tagore For You*, Kolkata, Visva-Bharati, 1984, p. 149.

Hail to Thee, O Mother![11] — 1879

Oh, don't ask me to sing. . .
who will rise today, who will work?
who is going to save
the face of the Mother?[12] — 1887

Walk alone, if nobody shows up
to respond to your call. . .[13] — 1905

Tagore lost his emotional self in 1917 in a confused gesture of humanism. One suspects that it was a temporary contradiction. For, sixteen years later, he recovered the simple patriotic emotion while dedicating the opening song of his *Tasher Desh* (1933) to Subhas Chandra Bose. Sri Aurobindo had been a hardcore nationalist since 1894. His nationalism never contradicted with his love for humanity. The fate of humanity depended on India's freedom. Sri Aurobindo's critics took him for a fanatic.

They were blind to the visional stuff, which lay hidden behind his aggressive editorials of the *Bande Mataram.* On 18 March 1908, he wrote:

> What is needed now is a band of spiritual workers whose *tapasyā* will be devoted to the liberation of India for the service of humanity. The few associations already started have taken another turn and devoted themselves to special and fragmentary work. We need an institution in which under the guidance of highly spiritual men workers will be trained for every field, workers for self-defence, workers for arbitration, for sanitation, for famine relief, for every species

---

11. *Rabindra Rachanabali,* vol. 4, W.B. Govt., 1987, p. 15, Lines translated by the author.
12. Ibid., p. 130, translated by the author.
13. *Gitobitan,* Visva-Bharati, Kolkata 1973, p. 244, translated by the author.

> of work which is needed to bring about the necessary conditions for the organization of Swaraj.[14]

But humanity was inseparably associated with his spiritual nationalism. In the editorial of 20 September 1907, he tells us that in true Nationalism which is an Indian contribution to the world, "there will be an essential equality between man and man, between caste and caste, between class and class, all being as Mr. Tilak has pointed out different but equal and united parts of the Virat Purusha as realized in the nation."[15] For Sri Aurobindo, it was not just rhetoric or an emotional appeal to initiate a revolutionary action. It was a living reality, a very special Indian nationalism, which was just a fleeting vision in Tagore. Sri Aurobindo saw the soul of Nationalism; it was not a thought, but a sight recorded in the editorial of 16 November 1907:

> Nationalism is an *avatara* and cannot be slain. Nationalism is a divinely appointed *śakti* of the Eternal and must do its God-given work before it returns to the bosom of the Universal Energy from which it came.[16]

He saw in Nationalism a spiritual movement for prophets, martyrs and heroes who stood in contradiction with the diplomats and "pinchbeck Machiavels". In Sri Aurobindo's nationalism, there is no scope for selfishness, greed and expansion of empire, which Tagore feared later in 1917. His nationalism opens our eyes to Sri Ramakrishna's contribution to the New Nationalism, which is going to help the whole of humanity:

---

14. Sri Aurobindo, *SABCL,* vol. 1, p. 765.
15. Ibid., p. 533.
16. Ibid., p. 600.

> A new era dates from his birth, an era in which the peoples of the earth will be lifted for a while into communication with God and spirituality becomes the dominant note of human life.[17]

This nationalism was a vision that was mistakenly seen as fanaticism by many intellectuals. For, vision is not intellectuality. The intellect cannot see the whole truth, the inner truth and the living reality hidden behind the surface self. One suspects it was a new interpretation of the Indian renaissance. Sri Aurobindo saw God in the movement and the intellectuals refused to accept it. They searched for the European symptoms of the renaissance. God woke up when wise men were speaking of an Indian renaissance. Tagore, the preacher of internationalism, belonged to the intellectual tradition, although he was not unaware of the spiritual view of life. Sri Aurobindo was thoroughly anti-intellectual in his choice of a vision of nationalism, which would ultimately benefit mankind. The preference for Sri Ramakrishna is a preference for intuition over intellect. He saw the rise of God in the movement and felt that Nationalism was God.

Although the Western glories were not unknown to them, both Tagore and Sri Aurobindo were quite often bold enough to claim the Indian superiority over Western gods of drama and poetry. Both were steeped in the Upanishads, the epics and the plays. Tagore was more prone to the West than Sri Aurobindo, but from time to time he was staunchly native and was more partial than Sri Aurobindo.

> In the Western dramas, human characters drown our attention in the vortex of their passions. Nature occasionally peeps out, but she is almost always a trespasser, who has to

---

17. Ibid., p. 801.

> offer excuses, or bow apologetically and depart. But in all our dramas which still retain their fame, such as *Mrit-Shakatika, Shakuntala, Uttara-ramcharita,* Nature stands on her own right, proving that she has her great function, to impart the peace of the eternal to human emotions. The fury of passion in two of Shakespeare's youthful poems is exhibited in conspicuous isolation. It is snatched away, naked, from the context of the All; it has not the green earth or the blue sky around it; it is there ready to bring to our view the fever which is in man's desires, and not the balm of health and repose which encircles it in the universe.[18]

Tagore should have spoken about the two different spirits, which worked behind the Shakespearean and the Kalidasian models. That would have made his criticism more balanced. Sri Aurobindo points out the basic difference between the Elizabethan and the Hindu plays in very clear terms, even though he is strongly indicating the cultural superiority of Hindu Drama.

> To the Hindu it would have seemed a savage and inhuman spirit that could take any aesthetic pleasure in the sufferings of an Oedipus or a Duchess of Malfi or in the tragedy of a Macbeth or an Othello. Partly this arose from the Divine tenderness of the Hindu nature, always noble, forbearing and gentle and at that time saturated with the sweet and gracious pity and purity which flowed from the soul of Buddha; but it was also the necessary result of the principle that aesthetic and intellectual pleasure is the first object of all poetic art.[19]

In Tagore, we do not see this immediate seizing of the points of difference. There is a digressive looseness in his prose. When he talks of Kalidasa's concentration on Nature and the lack of

18. *The English Writings of Rabindranath Tagore,* vol. II, p. 513.
19. Sri Aurobindo, *SABCL,* vol. 3, *The Harmony of Virtue*, p. 302.

that in Shakespeare, he is as strong in his comparative criticism as Sri Aurobindo and as acutely conscious of the Indian glory as the poet of *yoga*. Tagore passes from general to particular with the smoothness of a creative critic.

> Strangely enough, in Shakespeare's dramas, like those of Kalidasa, we find a secret vein of complaint against the artificial life of the king's court — the life of ungrateful treachery and falsehood. And almost everywhere, in his dramas, foreign scenes have been introduced in connection with some working of the life of unscrupulous ambition. It is perfectly obvious in *Timon of Athens* — but there Nature offers no message or balm to the injured soul of man. In *Cymbeline,* the mountainous forest and the cave appear in their aspect of obstruction to life's opportunities. These only seem tolerable in comparison with the vicissitudes of fortune in the artificial court life. In *As You Like It* the forest of Arden is didactic in its lessons. It does not bring peace, but preaches, when it says,
>
> Hath not old custom made this life more sweet
> Than that of painted pomp? Are not these words
> More free from peril than the envious court?[20]

Tagore goes on with his examples from *The Tempest, Macbeth, King Lear, Hamlet, Othello, The Merchant of Venice, Romeo and Juliet, Antony and Cleopatra* and *The Winter's Tale.* For Tagore, the Indian literature reflects a free individual, who looks at Nature to realize his soul beyond himself. Like Sri Aurobindo, Tagore is not afraid of talking about Shakespeare's limitations.

> I hope it is needless for me to say that these observations are not intended to minimize Shakespeare's great power as a dramatic poet, but to show in his works the gulf between

---

20. *The English Writings of Rabindranath Tagore,* vol. II, p. 516.

> Nature and human nature owing to the tradition of his race and time. It cannot be said that beauty of Nature is ignored in his writings; only he fails to recognize in them, the truth of the interpenetration of human life with the cosmic life of the world. We observe a completely different attitude of mind in the later English poets like Wordsworth and Shelley, which can be attributed in the main to the great mental change in Europe, at that particular period, through the influence of the newly discovered philosophy of India which stirred the soul of Germany and aroused the attention of other Western countries.[21]

Sri Aurobindo would have used the word psychic awareness in place of Tagore's phrase "mental change." But in both we see this fascination for the great Indian glories, like the Upanishads, the epics, the great Hindu plays and the Buddhist principles of life. And they were not exaggerating; they were giving us facts, inner and outer. As Sri Aurobindo is a better summariser of the two, let us observe the conclusive note to his masterful essay on Hindu Drama:

> If we expect a beautiful *White Devil* or a *Jew of Malta* from the Hindu dramatist, we shall be disappointed; he deals not in these splendid or horrible masks. If we come to him for a Lear or a Macbeth, we shall go away discontented; for these also are sublimities which belong to cruder civilizations and more barbarous national types; in worst crimes and utmost suffering as well as happiness and virtue, the Aryan was more civilized and temperate, less crudely enormous than the hard and earthy African peoples whom in Europe he only half moralized. If he seeks a Pere Goriot or a Madame Bovary, he will still fail in his quest; for though such types doubtless existed at all times among the mass of the people

21. Ibid., p. 517.

> with the large strain of African blood, Hindu art would have shrunk from poisoning the moral atmosphere of the soul by elaborate studies of depravity.[22]

The tonal difference is unmistakable. This and many passages from *The Foundations of Indian Culture* indicate Sri Aurobindo's disgust against the forceful imposition of Western superiority over things Indian. Tagore is mellow when he speaks of his native strength; Sri Aurobindo blends the mellow and the biting modes in his writings of the Baroda and the Calcutta phases. Later in his life, in Pondicherry, he throws away the razor, except in some occasional moments, when the bite is back without its old kick, as we see in his defence of Indian culture against the baseless criticism of William Archer. The Western views on Indian culture needed some revision in the early part of the twentieth century. Sri Aurobindo counter-attacks Archer by calling him a "new journalistic Apollo" and "devil's advocate,"[23] but after that calms down to concentrate on his defence by bringing in the logical texture.

> To the Indian mind, the least important part of religion is its dogma; the religious spirit matters, not the theological credo. On the contrary to the western mind a fixed intellectual belief is the most important part of a cult; it is its core meaning, it is the thing that distinguishes it from others.[24]

He rejects the stress of intellect, which is the basic feature of Western philosophy in general. He does not consider intellectual truth as the highest verity. Logic does not lead us to truth. Sri Aurobindo stresses on his basic conviction: "The supreme truths are neither the rigid conclusions of logical

---

22. Sri Aurobindo, *SABCL*, vol. 3, pp. 306-7.
23. Sri Aurobindo, *SABCL*, vol. 14, p. 94.
24. Ibid., p. 123.

reasoning nor the affirmations of credal statement, but fruits of the soul's inner experience."[25] Indian religion placed four necessities for humanity: a belief in the highest consciousness, the individual's need for self-preparation, a prescription of discipline for those aspiring for the highest consciousness and a general prescription for the not-yet-ready commoners to work out their way through a collective life.[26] In this way, Sri Aurobindo wishes his readers to know the real value of his native culture. Tagore is a confused nationalist, who sometimes fails to see the link between true nationalism and the true ideals of human unity.

Along with the oppositional nationalism of his days in Calcutta (1906-9), Sri Aurobindo was simultaneously talking of a new India and a new world beyond nationalism. By 1907, he began talking of the Indian freedom as an essential condition of the emancipation of the human race. He was then criticizing the distortion of the caste system in Hindu religion and the value of Vedanta, which sought to establish the divine unity of man in spirit. In "Asiatic Democracy," he explained the Asiatic reading of democracy, which India had to rediscover for herself.

> When man is free in spirit, all other freedom is at his command. When he is liberated from delusion, he perceives the divine equality of the world which fulfils itself through love and justice, and this perception transfuses itself into the law of government and society. When he has perceived the divine equality, he is brother to the whole world. . . .[27]

Sri Aurobindo was meaning a change in the human consciousness, although his expressive skill and vision were

---

25. Ibid., p. 124.
26. Ibid., p. 124-27.
27. Sri Aurobindo, *SABCL*, vol. 1, p. 759.

not at their highest heights in 1908. Back from the prison in the summer of 1909, he evolved further, showing distinct signs of a transition from nationalism to post-nationalism in his essay entitled "The Doctrine of Sacrifice" (*Karmayogin*). The essay speaks of the evolution of sacrifice, the gradual enlargement of the self from the smallest unit: from family to community, from community to nation, from nation to humanity. Only a few individuals have shown themselves ready for that last leap in consciousness. Sri Aurobindo's words hint at the evolutionary principles of the human consciousness.

> God prepares, but He does not hasten the ripening of the fruit before its season. A time will come when this also will be possible, but the time is not yet. Nor it would be well for humanity if it came before the other and lesser identification were complete . . . there is no great gain in rushing positions far ahead, while important points in the rear are uncaptured.[28]

About three years later, the oppositional nationalist has gone beyond his religion and nation. We now see him thinking of Man (the word includes woman too) living anywhere under the sun. By 1915, when he began serializing *The Human Cycle* and *The Ideal of Human Unity*, his India became just an important limb of his larger unit. Throughout the visional commentaries on the evolving planet and the possible contours of the future, Sri Aurobindo speaks quite often of the equal status of men and women working together on the high road to a new creation. The concept of the new woman creeps in here and there in his plays, poems, short fiction (*The Phantom Hour*) and non-fiction. The subaltern speaks through his texts, sometimes asserts his/her rights in an otherwise male dominated comedy like *The Viziers* of Bassora. Sri Aurobindo

28. Sri Aurobindo, *SABCL*, vol. II, p. 109.

goes back in Indian history to trace his/her free status in *The Foundations of Indian Culture.* Apart from his bold portrayal of a subaltern hero in *Baji Prabhou,* he repeatedly speaks of the need of uplifting the masses to hasten the reconstruction of a new world society. In *The Ideal of Human Unity,* Sri Aurobindo leaves behind his religion and nation in search of an ideal existence of man, a single world, where mankind will come to stand under one cosmic umbrella keeping intact their separate individualities and identities. He appreciates science and anticipates today's globalization as early as in 1915. He even hints at mixed marriages, which will hasten the death of "religionism" (aggressive Hinduism and aggressive Islam), the imperfect form of religion. The fact that the directors of *Veer Zara* and *Bombay* have imagined a love beyond religionism shows that the time is coming when religionism will have no access to the finer world of love. To imagine is to realize. What was once a blank prescience does not seem quite absurd in view of the social developments we see around us today. Sri Aurobindo believes that the human unity is a pressing need and therefore it is inevitable in the future. On 4 February 2007, Kolkata *HT* published a significant news under the caption: "46 nations line up to fight the heat." French President Jacques Chirac said: "The future of humanity demands it." *The Intergovernmental Panel on Climate Change's* report sparked calls for fast, planet-wide actions and was embraced by Europeans. "A total of 46 countries agreed to pursue plans for the new organization, and to hold their first meeting in Morocco this spring."[29]

Science is the great power of uniformity of thought and life and method. Sri Aurobindo reminds us that there can be

---

29. Kolkata *Hindusthan Times,* 4 February 2007, p. 14.

no such thing as national science, which is a thing common to all men in its conclusions. "The only difference that exists still is between the mind of the Occident and the mind of the Orient. But here too Asia is undergoing the shock of Europeanism and Europe is beginning to feel, however slightly, the reflux of Asiaticism. A common world-culture is the most probable outcome." There will be no block to centralization then. Even one of the most irrational aspects, the race sense, will be removed "by the closer intellectual, cultural and physical intercourse, which is inevitable in the not distant future."[30] The ultimate result must be the formation of a world state.

As Sri Aurobindo moves from one phase to another in the observation of Nature's slow march to unify man, at every step his voice rises up in defence of the individual, who is the leader of humanity. Then he speaks of the counter movements, which are bound to come at various stages making man stifled by the boredom of identity crisis. The social evolution of the human race is governed by three constant factors: individuals, communities of various types and mankind. Each seeks its own fulfilments and satisfaction, but each is compelled to develop them not independently but in relation to the others. Freedom is a necessity. Also, diversity is as necessary as unity for our true completeness. Sri Aurobindo ponders over the problems of centralization: social, legislative, administrative and economic. A new order is demanded by the new conditions, and so long as it is not created, there will be a transitional era of continued trouble or recurrent disorders, inevitable crisis through which Nature will shape out its future pattern. Sri Aurobindo insists on the need of military unification under the world state. "The international authority must hold under its command the sole trained military force

30. Sri Aurobindo, *SABCL*, vol. 15, p. 480.

in the world for the policing of the nations and also the sole disposal of the means of manufacturing arms and implements of war. National and private munition factories and arms factories must disappear."[31] At the back of his mind, Sri Aurobindo must be thinking of a better group controlling the world state, better in consciousness, and certainly there will be no George Bush as one of its members. Knowing well the failure of the League of Nations, Sri Aurobindo anticipates a slightly better performance by UNO. The formation of these two bodies has been hopeful signs for him and the right path to a proper international authority of the future. He observes that an imperfect organization like UNO should not start with stress on military force. Since industry and trade are now five-sixths of social life and the economic principles the governing principles of society, a world state, according to Sri Aurobindo, must initially focus on those aspects. While insisting on keeping the separate languages, he dreams of a common language becoming a reality in the future.

The world state will evolve, through breakings and makings. Sri Aurobindo cautions us against a more formidable danger than tyranny of the majority. He calls it "the tyranny of the whole, of the self-hypnotized mass over its constituent groups and units."[32] Obviously, he fears the suffocation of the individuals, without the freedom of which society cannot be progressive. Society is only the enlargement of the free individual. He appreciates the idea of freedom, equality and brotherhood, but insists that brotherhood exists only in the soul and by the soul. He further insists on a spiritual religion of humanity. Man is united by a secret spirit, a divine reality.

---

31. Ibid., p. 461.
32. Ibid., p. 485.

His business over here is to manifest that reality in material life.

Both in *The Human Cycle* and *The Ideal of Human Unity*, Sri Aurobindo tells us that the higher hope of humanity lies in the growing number of exceptional individuals, who will realize this truth and seek to develop it in themselves. It is certain that all humanity will not be able to achieve a rapid conversion. The hierarchy will be there in the gradation of consciousness. Sri Aurobindo says in *The Human Cycle*:

> This hierarchy would not mean as in our present vital living an egoistic domination of the undeveloped by the more developed, but a guidance of the younger by the elder brothers of the race and a constant working to lift them up to greater spiritual level and wider horizons.[33]

This may be possible only by a great widening of the self, the growth into a cosmic consciousness, by the sacrifice of the little ego. This will become easy if a person knows how to bring his/her psychic being to the front. The cover story of *India Today* (12 February 2007) presenting the profiles of 24 children shows us a few examples of the awakened psychic being in children. Damayanti Datta, the writer, calls it "inner compulsion to help others."[34] Sri Aurobindo would have called it the action of the psychic being. Whenever a single soul is liberated in any part of the world, "there is a tendency to an extension and even to an outburst of the same divine self-consciousness in other individual souls of our terrestrial humanity. . ."[35] The poetry of Whitman speaks of this great expansion as if to introduce the great age of Sri Aurobindo, where man and his material life are too precious for the new

33. Ibid., p. 253.

34. *India Today*, ed. Prabhu Chawla, 12 February 2007, p. 14.

35. Sri Aurobindo, *SABCL*, vol. 18, p. 40.

spirituality. Love and ego cannot live together. The entry of love means the exit of the small "I." The pressure of a new love is no utopia. Whitman's lines foreshadow the coming of those individuals.

> Camerado, I give you my hand!
> I give you my love more precious than money
> I give you myself before preaching and law;
> Will you give me yourself? Will you come travel with me?
> Shall we stick by each other as long as we live?[36]

Only poets can imagine or live out the future. Beyond this polluted and plundered planet lies the serene world, when man will learn to say "you" first, then "I." The reconstruction of the self is a certain way to the unification of the world. Many are working towards that goal from different parts of the world. Sri Aurobindo does not negative the possibility of a third great war. That might be the final pressure of Nature on humanity. Rabindranath Tagore was not quite practical in his views on human unity, even though he was always trying to find out ways to that. But, he also knew like Sri Aurobindo that the ego was a great obstruction to any kind of unity and that the expansion of the self would solve many problems relating to human unity.

---

36. *Leaves of Grass* (by Walt Whitman), Reader's Edition, ed. Harold W. Bloodgett and Sculley Bradley, University of London Press Ltd., 1965.

4

Education : An Integral Approach

UNLIKE the Mother and Tagore, Sri Aurobindo has not spoken much about the practical or material aspects of education. The Mother has compensated for Sri Aurobindo's silence and physical aloofness by building up a powerful educational centre in Pondicherry. Of course, there has always been Sri Aurobindo's authentic consent behind the Moher's theory of education. The material life is the basis of his *yoga* and he seems to have depended on the Mother for the details relating to the application of education in our material life.

Tagore, like the Mother, worked hard as a teacher, thinking out not just the ideological issues but also the prospects relating to the economic security of his pupils. The ideological issues have been identical: the development of the soul of man, the growth of beauty in the individual and above all the change of consciousness. If society is the enlargement of the individual, then both Tagore and Sri Aurobindo have struggled throughout their lives to hasten that enlargement.

Tagore's career as an educationist may be divided, according to Satyendranath Roy,[1] into three phases: (1) Pre-Santiniketan Days (1892-1901), (2) Pre-Visva-Bharati Santiniketan era (1901-18), and (3) Visva-Bharati period (1918-41). Most of Tagore's English writings had been pre-

---

1. Satyendranath Roy (ed.), *Rabindranather Chintajagat: Siksha Chinta Rachana Sankalon*, Calcutta, Granthalay, 2002.

shaped in Bengali. The famous pieces in English include *The Centre of Indian Culture* (1919), *An Eastern University* (1921), *The Visva-Bharati Ideal* (1923), *The School Master* (1924), *A Poet's School* (1926), *Ideal of Education* (1929), *My Educational Mission* (1931) and *Ideal of Indian University* (1934).

In the pre-Santiniketan period (1892-1901), Tagore held forth against both the British system and the indigenous private system, which were still prevalent in India. The major essay of this period entitled *Shikkhar Herfer* (1892) concentrates on two points in its criticism of British or colonial education: (1) the harmonization of life and education, and (2) the inevitability of the mother tongue in education. Tagore sees no life in colonial education. This essay is a prescience of Tagore's educational philosophy in its final shape: English is the language of utility, not the language of our emotion; the seed time of our life is wasted as we struggle to learn this language; this education has no link with our inner life; this education is to produce clerks not "man"; there is no place for joy in this education; it just strengthens our memory and weakens our imagination. Among the supporters of this view was Bankim Chandra Chatterjee whom Sri Aurobindo appreciated two years later as the most expressive interpreter of Bengali native culture.[2] Sri Aurobindo, himself divorced from the native soil, realized the truth and echoed Tagore in the following passage:

> The language which a man speaks and which he has never learned, is the language of which he has the nearest sense and in which he expresses himself with the greatest fulness, subtlety and power. He may neglect, he may forget it, but he will always retain for it a hereditary aptitude, and it will

2. Sri Aurobindo, *SABCL*, vol. 3, see the essays on Bankim Chandra Chatterjee, pp. 75-102.

> always continue for him the language in which he has the safest chance of writing with originality and ease. To be original in an acquired tongue is hardly feasible. . . . It has something unnatural and spurious about it like speaking with a stone in the mouth or walking upon stilts. Bankim and Madhusudan, with their overflowing originality, must have very acutely felt the tameness of their English work. The one wrote no second English poem after the *Captive Lady,* the other no second English novel after *Rajmohan's Wife.*[3]

Santiniketan School was founded in December 1901. Tagore had then a vague perception of ancient Indian *Tapovan.* It was an idealistic image formed in a poet's consciousness. The image was mirrored in the *Naibedya* (*Offerings,* 1901) poems.

In 1906, just a year after the partition of Bengal, Tagore was strongly nationalistic in all his writings on education. His educational ideas verged on Internationalism from 1917 onwards. When the Visva-Bharati phase started in 1918 it was a distinct call for global education instead of a pure Indian education. The ideal of Visva-Bharati was the fusion of spiritual and scientific education, the blend of national and international education. In 1924, a village school was founded in Sriniketan (*Shikshasatra*) as the second experiment of Tagore, the educationist. It was a direct action related to the secondary aim of education, the aim of securing jobs. By 1924, Tagore became a champion of mass education. Tagore knew, like Sri Aurobindo and the Mother, that the aim of livelihood is related to our wants and necessities and that the aim of life is "completeness," which is above all necessities. The aim of human life and the aim of education are the same. It is just here that we see the meeting place of Tagore and Sri

3. Ibid., p. 90.

Aurobindo. Education keeps alive the quest for completeness, the quest for endless becoming. Like Sri Aurobindo, Tagore was aware of the value of man in relation to society; he also knew like the sage of Pondicherry that the education should be complete and integral:

> . . . Our education should be in full touch with our complete life, economical, intellectual, aesthetic, social and spiritual; and our educational institutions should be in the very heart of our society, connected with it by the living bonds of varied co-operations. For true education is to realize at every step how our training and knowledge have organic connection with our surroundings.[4]

Time and again, Tagore returns to the issue of integrality — not of course with the word "integral" — and there is always a consideration for the mass and the elite, the spiritual and the mundane, the high and the low:

> Our ancient *tapovanas,* or forest schools, which were our natural universities, were not shut off from the daily life of the people. Masters and students gathered fruit and fuel, and took their cattle out to graze, supporting themselves by the work of their own hands. Spiritual education was a part of the spiritual life itself, which comprehended all life. Our centre of culture should not only be the centre of the intellectual life of India, but the centre of her economic life also. I must co-operate with the villages round it, cultivate land, breed cattle, spin cloths, press oil from oil seeds; it must produce all the necessaries devising the best means, using the best materials, and calling science to its aid. Its very existence should depend upon the success of its industrial activities carried out on the co-operative principle, which will unite the teachers and students and villagers of

4. Sisir Kumar Das (ed.), *The English Writings of Rabindranath Tagore,* vol. II, 2001, p. 469.

> the neighbourhood in a living and active bond of necessity. This will also give us a practical industrial training, whose motive force is not the greed of profit.[5]

Tagore then passes on to the ideal, which has to be felt and realized through our proper attitude to life. He comes directly to the Aurobindonian world when he speaks of "our conscious relationship with the Infinite, and the lasting power of the Eternal in the passing moments of our life."[6] Sri Aurobindo's poetry of the early years records this realization in moments when the poet stands before the sea or a tree by the beach or before the sun going down into the sea in the far away horizon.

Sri Aurobindo's theory of education is directly related to his new *yoga,* the Integral Yoga, and to his theory of man as a multiple being. He knows that every layer of the being has to be trained to achieve a synthesis of knowledge within us. Like Tagore, Sri Aurobindo began with a strong stress on national education and then went on to explain the relevance of national education to humanity in general He was never fanatically national, as the following passage from *Bande Mataram* (24 February 1908) confirms:

> We must therefore save for India all that she has stored up of knowledge, character and noble thought in her immemorial past. We must acquire for her the best knowledge that Europe can give her and assimilate it to her own peculiar type of national temperament. We must introduce the best methods of teaching humanity has developed, whether modern or ancient. And all these we must harmonize into a system which will be impregnated with the spirit of self-reliance so as to build-up men and not machines — national men, able men, men fit to carve out a

5. Ibid., p. 568.
6. Ibid.

> career for themselves by their own brain-power and resource, fit to meet the shocks of life and breast the waves of adventure. So shall the Indian people cease to sleep and become once more a people of heroes, patriots, originators, so shall it become a nation and no longer a disorganized mass of men.[7]

The passage speaks of Sri Aurobindo's commitment to the cause of India during his life in Calcutta. Sri Aurobindo's credo as an educationist seems to have been based on a concrete philosophy. Let us listen to his ideology:

> The first principle of true teaching is that nothing can be taught. The teacher is not an instructor or task-master, he is a helper and a guide. His business is to suggest and not to impose. He does not actually train the pupil's mind, he only shows him how to perfect his instruments of knowledge and helps and encourages him in the process. He does not impart knowledge to him, he shows how to acquire knowledge for himself. He does not call forth the knowledge that is within; he only shows him where it lies and how it can be habituated to rise to the surface. . . . The second principle is that the mind has to be consulted in its own growth. The idea of hammering the child into the shape desired by the parent or teacher is a barbarous and ignorant superstition. It is he himself who must be induced to expand in accordance with his own nature. There can be no greater error than for the parent to arrange beforehand that his son shall develop particular qualities, capacities, ideas, virtues, or be prepared for a prearranged career.[8]

Sri Aurobindo wishes the child to have a free growth. This idea is part of his existential philosophy: a child's growth is unforeseen, as an invisible guide within is shaping his/her

7. Sri Aurobindo, *SABCL*, vol. 1, p. 718.
8. Sri Aurobindo, *SABCL*, vol. 17, The Hour of God, p. 204.

destiny. The parents or the teachers should not obstruct the law of his nature, which Sri Aurobindo calls *dharma.* "It is a selfish tyranny over a human soul and a wound to the nation, which loses the benefit of the best that a man could have given it and is forced to accept instead something imperfect and artificial, second-rate, perfunctory and common."[9]

Sri Aurobindo considers "heredity" and "surroundings" when he comes to his third principle of education. A child should not be uprooted from his environment. If anything has to be supplied from outside, it must be placed before the child as an offer, not imposed on his/her mind. He appreciates the progressive ideas regarding the education of a child and it is clear that he is appreciating the Western educators, who see in the child a deeper self, a psychic entity. In chapter three of *The Human Cycle,* he says:

> These new educational methods are on the straight way to this truer dealing. The closer touch attempted with the psychical entity behind the vital and physical mentality and an increasing reliance on its possibilities must lead to the ultimate discovery that man is inwardly a soul and a conscious power of the Divine and that the evocation of this real man within is the right object of education and indeed of all human life if it would find and live according to the hidden Truth and deepest law of its own being.[10]

He contradicts the idea preached in the totalitarian states that the individual does not exist and that only the life of the community matters. Both Tagore and Sri Aurobindo emphasize the role of the individual in building a sound collective life. In the Pondicherry period, in the second decade of the twentieth century, the Lover of Humanity explains his concept of

9. Ibid.

10. Sri Aurobindo, *SABCL,* vol. 15, *Social Writings,* p. 28.

Nationalism more clearly than his earlier efforts in Calcutta (1906-10). The tone is quiet; the vision is certain in the following passage:

> A national culture, a national religion, a national education may still be useful things provided they do not interfere with the growth of human solidarity on the one side and individual freedom of thought and conscience and development on the other; for they give form to the communal soul and help it to add its quota to the sum of human advancement; but a State education, a State religion, a State culture are unnatural violences.[11]

In *War and Self-Determination,* Sri Aurobindo speaks again of the value of the child as a free spirit. He was in the ancient patriarchal concept "the live property of the father," his created image of himself. The father claimed God's property for himself:

> He had the right to make of him what he willed, and not what the being of the child really was within; to train and shape and cut him according to the parental ideas and not rear him according to his own nature's deepest needs; to bind him to the paternal career or the career chosen by the parent and not that to which his nature and capacity and inclination pointed; to fix for him all the critical turning-points of his life even after he had reached maturity. In education the child was regarded not as a soul meant to grow, but as brute psychological stuff to be shaped into a fixed mould by the teacher. We have travelled to another conception of the child as a soul with a being, a nature and capacities of his own who must be helped to find them, to find himself, to grow into their maturity, into a fullness of physical and vital energy and the utmost breadth, depth,

11. Ibid., p. 283.

> and height of his emotional, his intellectual and his spiritual being.[12]

Sri Aurobindo is speaking here about the integral development of the child as a free traveller whose guide remains within him waiting to be activised. Any interference from outside blocks the growth and evolution of the psychic entity. Sri Aurobindo's theory of education is directly linked up with his *yoga* of perfection. The aim is too high even for a Rousseau or a Gandhi. For, morality and a faint perception of Beauty or God were not the goal of Sri Aurobindo.

Only in Tagore's ideal of education there is a clue to the beautification of man and this earth and the dream of the God-touch in human life. This dream of Tagore, even though it is restricted to the mental prescience of the Supramental, links him up with Sri Aurobindo, who speaks of a complete education: mental, vital, physical, psychic and spiritual. The Mother completes the map of this fivefold system of education. It is interesting that both Tagore and Sri Aurobindo did not actively participate in sports. But then, both were aware of the necessity of physical education. Tagore wished the students to train their body with the help of natural activities:

> By training of the body I do not mean physical exercise. By that I mean those works, which we usually do with the help of the body. That educates the body and drives away its inertia. Those works unite the body and the mind. And the unification helps the development of both.[13]

---

12. Ibid., p. 605.
13. *Santiniketan Patrika,* July 1925, Passage Quoted by Satyendranath Roy in *Siksha Chinta,* p. 215, translated by the author from Bengali.

On 30 December 1948, only about two years before his passing, Sri Aurobindo's message[14] for the *Bulletin of Physical Education* verges on the Mother's philosophy of physical education as the art of infusing consciousness into the body. Sri Aurobindo sees the revival of the Greek spirit in the re-establishment of the Olympiad as an international institution and also in the mass appeal of sports, games and athletics in his own time. Both the poets stayed away from the sportsground and yet both agreed that no education was complete without the education of the body.

---

14. Sri Aurobindo, *SABCL*, vol. 16, *The Supramental Manifestation*, pp. 1-4.

5

Towards a New Aesthetics

TAGORE'S immediate fame was not due to his "global" awareness. It was the "native" stuff that made him popular all over the world. He was seeking to discover ancient India for a new audience. His language was new and he knew how to think it out again for the future and how many things of the old world had no relevance to the present and the future. It is this awareness of the ever-progressive new that relates him to Sri Aurobindo. Unlike Sri Aurobindo, he wished to recreate the basics of Indian spirituality and mysticism. His poetry was often simple and sweet and people were athirst for the stuff, the inward look in poetry and in the daily life. The Renascent India took him fondly in her arms as a sweet reminder. His earth-oriented theory of art and aesthetics was a sensation in those moments of reawakening. While Tagore and Sri Aurobindo were recording their views on art and poetry and writing their best poetry almost simultaneously (barring *Savitri*, which Sri Aurobindo began writing anew after Tagore's death), Sri Aurobindo's words were known only to a small group of readers. It was good for the readers that they had the foretaste of the mighty works of Sri Aurobindo in the popular Bengali writer.

One was a public writer; the other lived in isolation and above the artistic ego. Sri Aurobindo was conscious about his achievement — in fact, a little too conscious, but he could ignore easily the call for publicity and awards. His life and the Mother's life falsified the popular belief that the artist could never surrender. Both were supreme artists and both kept the Divine above everything else. Their lives were two wonderful pieces of art. Tagore could only aspire for that status. He did. That is why Sri Aurobindo chose him in *The Future Poetry* to verify the inward turn in modern poetry.

> His (Tagore's) work is a constant music of the overpassing of the borders, a chart-filled realm in which the subtle sounds and lights of the truth of the spirit give new meanings to the finer subtleties of life.[1]

Tagore learnt to write the poetry of incantation easily, because he was steeped in the Upanishads. The individual talent boldly went forward with his historical sense to see life in a new way, "to build bridges of visioned light and rhythm between the infinite and eternal and the mind and soul and life of man."[2] Sri Aurobindo attaches great value to this fusion of Spirit and Life in the poetry of Tagore, Whitman, A.E., Meredith and Yeats. Tagore's poetry indicates a turning point in the history of poetry, a moving away from the mere exterior to the finer subtleties of inner life.

How conscious was Tagore himself as a writer of incantatory verse or as a revealer of the secret self in man? In "What is Art?," we get a clear view of his concept of art and the theory of the surplus. He distinguishes between the physical man and the personal man before introducing his theory of the surplus. The personal man wishes to find something to fulfil his needs of love. This world lies beyond the necessities of man. The personal man is the highest in man. "And it has personal relations of its own with the great world, and comes

1. Sri Aurobindo, *SABCL*, vol. 9, *The Future Poetry*, p. 229.
2. Ibid.

to it for something to satisfy personality."[3] Science has no access to that mysterious world, where utility is missing. This world cannot be analysed and can only be felt. This is the world of Art, where the immaterial has a king-size status.

> The most important distinction between the animal and man is this, that the animal is very nearly bound within the limits of its necessities, the greater part of its activities being necessary for its self-preservation and the preservation of race. Like a retail shopkeeper, it has no large profit from its trade of life; the bulk of its earnings must be spent in paying back the interest to its bank. Most of its resources are employed in the mere endeavour to live. But man, in life's commerce is a big merchant. He earns a great deal more than he is absolutely compelled to spend. Therefore there is a vast excess of wealth in man's life, which gives him the freedom to be useless and irresponsible to a great measure. There are large outlying tracts, surrounding his necessities, where he has objects that are ends in themselves.[4]

This "surplus" is the source of Art, because the emotional efflux must find outlet of expression. This "surplus" is Greek to the world of science, which is just material. The personal man has been expelled from the world of science. In a revealing passage Tagore observes:

> Our emotions are the gastric juices, which transform this world of appearance into the more intimate world of sentiments. On the other hand, the outer world has its own juices, having their various qualities, which excite our emotional activities. This is called in our Sanskrit rhetoric *rasa,* which signifies outer juices having their response in the inner juices of our emotions. And a poem, according to

3. Sisir Kumar Das (ed.), *The English Writings of Rabindranath Tagore,* vol. II, New Delhi, Sahitya Akademi, p. 349.

4. Ibid., p. 351.

> it, is a sentence or sentences containing juices, which stimulate the juices of emotion. It brings to us ideas, vitalized by feelings, ready to be made into the life-stuff of our nature.[5]

Science can easily explain things by analysis and experiment. But, how can we express the personal man in us? Facts are useless, impotent, often stark lies in the world of love. The laws of science and the laws of emotion are two different things. The personal man deals with taste. Only tasting can help us realize the taste.

> Therefore the Sanskrit rhetoricians say, in poetry we have to use words which have got the proper taste — which do not merely talk, but conjure up pictures and sing. For, pictures and songs are not merely facts — they are personal facts. They are not only themselves, but ourselves also. They defy analysis and they have immediate access to our hearts.[6]

But, man also expresses his personality in the material world, where self-expression is not his primary aim. Our consciousness then remains on a low plane. As love and other emotions creep in, our consciousness expands and seeks the medium of Art. For Tagore, our true life is reflected in Art. He unites his voice with Sri Aurobindo when he says:

> Man is true, where he feels his infinity, where he is divine, and the divine is the creator in him. Therefore with the attainment of his truth he creates. For he can truly live in his own creation and make out of God's world his own world. . . . If man could only listen to the voice that rises from the heart of his own creation, he would hear the same message that came from the Indian sage of the ancient time:

---

5. Ibid., p. 353.
6. Ibid., p. 356.

> "Hearken to me, ye children of the Immortal, dwellers of the heavenly worlds, I have known the Supreme Person who comes as light from the dark beyond."[7]

Sri Aurobindo's theory of mantric poetry speaks of this voice of God as a reality in the creation of true poetry. He too gets the idea from the poetry of ancient India. Tagore and Sri Aurobindo, the two practising poets, have all the time been aware of the native tradition, which had seen "enjoyment" as the soul of literature. Of course, it is a disinterested enjoyment. The Sanskrit word *nishkama* means an absolute disinterestedness. How can "enjoyment" be a pure activity? Let us listen to Sri Aurobindo:

> The world is a movement of God in His own being; we are the centres and knots of divine consciousness which sum up and support the processes of His movement. The world is His play with His own self-conscious delight, He who alone exists, infinite, free and perfect; we are the self-multiplications of that conscious delight, thrown out into being to be His playmates. The world is a formula, a rhythm, a symbol-system expressing God to Himself in His own consciousness — it has no material existence but exists only in his consciousness and self-expression; we, like God, are in our inward being that which is expressed, but in our outward being terms of that formula, notes of that rhythm, symbols of that system. Let us lead forward God's system, play out His play, work out His formula, execute His harmony, express Him through ourselves in His system. This is our joy and our self-fulfilment; to this end we who transcend and exceed the universe, have entered into universe existence.[8]

---

7. Ibid., pp. 359-60.
8. Sri Aurobindo, *SABCL*, vol. 17, p. 50.

This is a subtler observation than Tagore's, but the basic thematic similarity is unmistakable. *Ananda* is the keyword in Sri Aurobindo's aesthetics. This is directly linked up with the theory of ancient Indian *rasa,* which stands for an integral aesthetic experience. Sri Aurobindo does not stick to the ancient rhetoricians; he sees an evolving aesthetics with the evolution of man's consciousness. What was there in the past is certainly very interesting; what is coming in the future is more fascinating. This prophetic note in Sri Aurobindo's theory of poetry gives a new dimension to his aesthetics and makes him a theoretician of tomorrow.

> This poetry will speak of new things and of old things in a new way and with a new voice, not by any exclusion or diminution of its province, but by a great heightening above, a great intimacy within, a great enlargement and wideness around, a vision of inmost things and therefore a changed vision of the world and life and the untold potentialities of the soul's experience.[9]

Sri Aurobindo is thinking of an art and poetry, which will be in harmony with a new world, a new creation. He is not thinking of a limited spirituality, a half-hearted flirtation with the Spirit; he is dreaming of the highest consciousness, which will give birth to the greatest poetry.

> In the greatest art and poetry there should be something of the calm of the impersonal basing and elevating the effort and struggle of the personality; something of the largeness of the universal releasing and harmonizing the troubled concentrations of the individual existence; something of the sense of the transcendent raising the inferior, ignorant and

---

9. Sri Aurobindo, *SABCL,* vol. 9, p. 251.

> uncertain powers of life towards a greater strength and light and *Ananda*.[10]

The change of consciousness initiates a change in poetry. The form of the new poetry will not be pre-conceived. The Spirit will create the form, only if the overactive intellect does not interfere in its natural work.

> Nature creates perfectly because she creates directly out of life and is not intellectually self-conscious, the spirit will create perfectly because it creates directly out of self and is spontaneously supra-intellectually all-conscious.[11]

Sri Aurobindo, the spiritual existentialist, knows well the value of the individual personality. His *yoga* does not seek to abolish what Tagore calls the personal man. Every person has his own personal way of enjoying either the Divine or His scattered rays. Therefore, Tagore's personal man will remain relevant to the poetry of the future. The following passage echoes Sri Aurobindo's theory of art in the usual style of Tagore:

> And this consciousness of the infinite, in the personal man, ever strives to make its expressions immortal and to make the whole world its own. In Art, the person in us is sending its answers to the Supreme Person, who reveals Himself to us in a world of endless beauty across the lightness world of facts.[12]

The presence of the personal man in every poet will lead to varieties of experience in the poetry of the future. For Tagore and Sri Aurobindo, life is perpetual creation. The Eternal is being manifested progressively. And this life is extremely important, a chance for new discoveries, a manifold

10. Ibid., p. 252.
11. Ibid., p. 262.
12. *The English Writings of Rabindranath Tagore*, vol. II, p. 362.

opportunity to discover the mighty rhythms in our upward and inward march. The aspiration in Tagore is quite Aurobindonian, as we can see in the following passage:

> Let us express our infinite in everything around us, in works we do, in things we use, in men with whom we deal, in the enjoyment of the world with which we are surrounded. Let our soul permeate our surroundings and create itself in all things, and show its fulness by fulfilling needs of all times. This life of ours has been filled with the gifts of the divine giver.[13]

Like Sri Aurobindo, Tagore knows that joy and love are the two ways to the Supreme and that the intellect is partial knowledge. The poets and the artists of the future will depend more on joy and love and less on the intellect. The hidden vast is beyond the range of the intellect. The poets of tomorrow will turn their eyes from outside to the self of man. They will not be satisfied by a mere cultured poetry dealing with finer things of the surface. The spirit will turn to its own intuitive will and vision. Sri Aurobindo sees a great possibility in the lyric form, which is a moment of heightened soul experience. He draws our notice to its very wide range and flexibility. He was surely thinking of the possibilities opened up by Tagore and Whitman in the lyrical mould. Let us listen to Sri Aurobindo's prophecy, which keeps the memory of Tagore alive:

> It is therefore in the lyric nearest to the freshness of an original impulse that a new spirit in poetry is likely to become aware of itself and feel out for its right ways of expression and to discover with the most adaptable freedom and variety its own essential motives and cadences, first forms and

13. Ibid., p. 372.

> simpler structures before it works out victoriously its greater motions or ampler figures in narrative and drama.[14]

Sri Aurobindo's aesthetic vision considers the future drama with reference to the inwardization of literature in future. He is surely thinking of the dramatic trends in Tagore, Yeats and Maeterlink. The success of Tagore's lyrical plays puts a significant question before us: will the drama remain an objective art in the future? Many of the speeches from Tagore's characters are just records of dream voyages of self-discovery. The change of consciousness will create new forms of drama and fiction. Speech will reflect the consciousness, and literature of the surface will lose its value in a spiritual society. Tagore's greatest contribution to the Bengali language and literature is this. He is a pioneer of a new poetry, a new aesthetics and a new language. He is also the most authentic forerunner of Sri Aurobindo's aesthetics and lyric poetry. Unlike Tagore, Sri Aurobindo does not speak in general about the poetry of higher consciousness. He maps the consciousness tiers, gives names to the ascending planes of consciousness, characterizes them, and initiates a group of poets to write poetry as *mantra* of the Real. But that does not minimize the stature of the great Bengali poet. Sri Aurobindo simply adds some more details to the aesthetic philosophy of Tagore, whose theory of surplus has a distinct link with Sri Aurobindo's theory of mantric poetry or poetry of incantation. In a striking passage in "What is Art?," Tagore virtually comes very close to the secret, which Sri Aurobindo calls "the soul of the emotion."[15] That is the essence of poetry as *mantra*. Let us examine the passage as an introduction to Sri Aurobindo's overhead aesthetics. Tagore catches the essence:

14. Sri Aurobindo, *SABCL*, vol. 9, pp. 258-59.
15. Ibid., p. 15.

> The principal creative forces, which transmute things into our living structure, are emotional forces. A man, where he is religious, is a person, but not where he is a pure theologian. His feeling for the divine is creative. But his mere knowledge of the divine cannot be formed into his own essence because of this lack of emotional fire.[16]

Theology invites the interference of the thinking mind, blocking the natural emotional centre, the psychic being, which leads us to even higher provinces of inspiration. The finer the quality of the emotion, the greater the level of inspiration. Sri Aurobindo has charted out the levels of inspiration, starting from the psychic and then moving up the ladder reaching to the highest summit of the mind, that is, the Overmind, which stands as a gateway to a new species beyond man, which he calls, the Supermind. According to Sri Aurobindo the ladder goes up like the following:

1. the Higher mind
2. the Illumined Mind
3. the Intuition
4. the Overmind

These are the spiritual planes, generally termed by him as the overhead planes, which have gone to the making of his overhead aesthetics. Poetry, according to Sri Aurobindo, becomes *mantra* only when the poet draws his inspiration from the highest summit of the mind, the Overmind, or the very high Intuition, which is nearly verging on the Overmind.

> The *mantra* as I have tried to describe it in *The Future Poetry* is a word of power and light that comes from the Overmind inspiration or from the very high plane of intuition. Its characteristics are a language that conveys infinitely more than the mere surface sense of the words seems to indicate,

16. *The English Writings of Rabindranath Tagore,* vol. II, p. 352.

> a rhythm that even means more than the language and is born out of the Infinite and disappears into it. . . .[17]

This Overmind inspiration is very rare even in the world's greatest poetry and there are only a few portions or passages in all poetic literature that offer at least some sparks or flashes of the thing. The Overmind plane contains much of the elements of the Supramental and the *Sachchidananda* consciousness, because it is very close to those areas above the mind. It expresses the cosmic consciousness, which we see so often in the poetry of Whitman, Tagore and Sri Aurobindo. The full Overmind inspiration in poetry is extremely rare. Sometimes, it is just a flash on a line like Wordsworth's "The winds come to me from the fields of sleep."[18] It may colour the substance of the line or its style or both the theme and the manner. Marlowe's lines on Helen in *Doctor Faustus* have nothing of spirituality in them. But, Sri Aurobindo feels the authentic touch of the Overmind in the style of those lines:

> Was this the face that launched a thousand ships
> And burnt the topless towers of Ilium?[19]

Mantric poetry is the basis of Sri Aurobindo's theory poetry and the essential aspect of his overhead aesthetics, which he believes, will be the aesthetics of future poetry. Sri Aurobindo quotes Marlowe's lines in a letter written to his poet-disciple, K.D. Sethna, and draws his notice to the "subtle something"

---

17. K.D. Sethna (ed.), *Overhead Poetry: Poems with Sri Aurobindo's Comments,* Pondicherry, Sri Aurobindo International Centre of Education, 1972, p. 12.

18. Francis Turner Palgrave (ed.), *The Golden Treasury of the Best Songs and Lyrical Poems in the English Language,* Calcutta, Oxford University Press, 1976, 1998.

19. Christopher Marlowe, *Doctor Fanstus,* Act V, Scene 1, quoted by Sri Aurobindo in a letter to K.D. Sethna, see *Overhead Poetry,* p. 53.

that marks "the language and feeling of the lines."[20] Tagore was quite deliberate in his use of the higher inspirations both in his substance and style. But, the did not offer a theory of poetry in such a detailed manner.

20. Ibid.

6

Tagore's Poetry
The Psychic and the Great Foreknowledge

APART from his frequent access to the psychic province, Tagore seems to have an authentic prescience of the Supernature. There is a wonderful guesswork in the poem entitled *Premer Abhishek* (*Love's Coronation*).

> There I stay full of Light
> like a god of eternal youth,
> there my beauty is boundless,
> there you've offered me your nature
> O, the Lover of all things!
> There I've as my companions
> the Sun, the Moon and the Stars.
> Wearing new clothes they sing to me
> newer and newer songs
> with newer and newer meanings,
> O my eternal friend, who lies everywhere![1]

How could Tagore anticipate this wonderful realization? Sri Aurobindo's explanation in *The Life Divine* sheds light on that foreknowledge:

> An aspiration, a demand for the supreme and total delight of existence is there secretly in the whole make of our being, but it is disguised by the separation of our parts of nature

1. Translated by the author, vol. 1 — *Rabindra Rachanabali*, 1980, Kolkata, W.B. Govt., p. 566.

> and their differing urge and obscured by their inability to conceive or seize anything more than a superficial pleasure. In the body-consciousness this demand takes shape as a need of bodily happiness, in our life-parts as a yearning for life-happiness, a keen vibrant response to joy and rapture of many kinds and to all surprise of satisfaction; in the mind it shapes into a ready reception of all forms of mental delight; on a higher level it becomes apparent in the spiritual mind's call for peace and divine ecstasy. This trend is founded in the truth of the being; for *Ananda* is the very essence of the *Brahman*, it is the supreme nature of the omnipresent Reality.[2]

Quite often, Tagore expresses the pleasures of his mind and body, feels the thrill and surprise as a borderline poet. And what expressions! He catches the moments in the form of mystic poetry, as a prescience of the ecstasy of tomorrow. Sri Aurobindo uses the prophetic future tense for the commoner; the aspirant soul is seen to be slowly moving towards the Infinite. Tagore uses the future tense as his own foretaste of the all-fulfilling peaks of the Supernature. Let me attempt a translation of a few lines from his *Gitimalya*:

> One day
> thousands of lotus
> will release their petals,
> the great Honey cannot be hidden
> for ever.
>
> Whose eye will wake up
> in the vast sky
> calling me out
> into the wide silence?
> Nothing will be there
> between you and I

---

2. Sri Aurobindo, *SABCL*, vol. 19, The Life Divine, pp. 989-90.

the great death under your feet
will bring me the supreme reward![3]

In poem after poem, from the beginning of his life till its close, the flame goes on burning with short-lived diversions here and there on small things of material life. His poetry speaks mostly of a sweet or painful separation, and even when he speaks of women or nature or human sorrows and joys, there is a refined aestheticism ligting up his common themes. Tagore seems to have been a fallen god in the form of a visiting poet on earth with the mission of changing man's attitude to earth. There are times when his poetry reveals his technique of spiritual practice or *sadhana*, the technique of constant remembrance of the Divine. Poetry then becomes an accompaniment to *sadhana*.

I'll utter your name under various pretences,
alone I'll speak within under the shadows.
I'll speak without speech,
without hoping for a return,
with the smiles and tears.

I'll utter your name
without thinking of its utility;
that will make me full,
like the child who calls his mother
being intoxicated by the name,
who calls his mother
because he is thrilled by his own call.[4]

The psychic sadness has taken wonderful shapes in Tagore. It is everywhere in Tagore's songs, in the shorter and longer lyrics, and also in the songs inside his "vital" plays and dance

---

3. Translated by the author, vol. 2 — *Rabindra Rachanabali*, 1982, Kolkata, pp. 313-14.

4. Ibid., p. 318.

dramas. He wishes to see the Divine's face before he goes, in the evening twilight, in the light of this life or he wishes to chase Him like young Aurobindo in life after life with the memory that he had failed to seize Him in the previous life. Tagore knows that it is not always a sweet game, but there is no indifference from the other side as the blows are frequent.

He pines for a love that will link him up with the Divine. He greets the thorns in the hope of a bright blossoming in the future. He dreams that all pains will wake up to a colourful rose. The light spread across the sky makes him eager for an inevitable union. Then there are strange moments when he feels that much before his destination the lamps have gone out and most of the flowers have fallen down from his tray. Every now and then, a deep sense of gratitude wells up from the fountainhead of the Spirit. Even when the Luminous has left him, as in the later poems, memories come back to him in different shapes and contours.

Sri Aurobindo never says that anybody from the mental province can guess the Supermind. We have to read his prose very carefully:

> It would be difficult for the normal unilluminated or untransformed mental conception to express or enter into something that is based on so different a consciousness with a radically different awareness of things; even if they were seen or conceived by some enlightenment or opening of vision, another language than the poor abstract counters used by our mind would be needed to translate them into terms by which their reality could at all become seizable by us.[5]

Tagore's capacity is certainly higher than what Sri Aurobindo calls "the normal unilluminated or untransformed mental

5. Sri Aurobindo, *SABCL,* vol. 19, pp. 919-20.

conception." Tagore's is not the ordinary human mental conception. It is rather an extraordinary human mental conception. That helps him guess the Supernature here and there in his fine mystic poetry. Sri Aurobindo goes on to clarify the issue:

> . . . it is only when we have already had experience of a higher intermediate consciousness that any terms attempting to describe supramental being could convey a true meaning to our intelligence; for then, having experienced something akin to what is described, we could translate an inadequate language into a figure of what we knew. If the mind cannot enter into the nature of Supermind, it can look towards it through these high and luminous approaches and catch some reflected impression of the Truth, the Right, the Vast which is the native kingdom of the free spirit.[6]

As Tagore frequently draws his inspiration from the higher mind, the illumined mind and the intuition, the guesswork becomes easier for him.

> In many a morning and eve thy footsteps have been heard and thy messenger has come within my heart and called me in secret.[7]

As if to explain the poetic aim of Tagore or justify his mental perception of the Supramental, Sri Aurobindo observes:

> An Unknowable which appears to us in many states and attributes of being, in many forms of consciousness, in many activities of energy, this is what Mind can ultimately say about the existence which we ourselves are and which we see in all that is presented to our thought and senses. It is in

6. Ibid., p. 920.
7. *Gitanjali,* poem no. 46.

> and through those states, those forms, those activities that we have to approach and know the Unknowable.[8]

That is Tagore's poetic endeavour: to catch the eternal in finite forms. How far he succeeded is another question. But, a curious blend of poetry and *sadhana* makes him an extremely interesting person. The point is: when he can open the psychic so easily in poem after poem, especially in the early and middle part of his life, it is natural that he is automatically inviting the Supermind principles to invade him through his mental filter. For, the psychic inevitably pushes us towards that Supreme Reality, where we have that integrating Light, the consummating Force, the wide entry into the supreme *ananda*. Moving in the hemisphere between the Man and the *rishi*, Tagore seems to have been enjoying his half-thoughts and at the same time pining for the supreme status lying beyond his reach. He seems to have understood or even realized that nothing should come between him and the Divine. But things came between them and that made him sad. That is not quite the usual Aurobindonian melancholy. But then, it was very real, very intense. Surely, he sought release in lovely lyrics; he spoke it out; he spoke about his faulty choice. He rose and then went to sleep. When he rose again he thought of the greater possibilities, which had come his way. The cry came back from time to time, the cry for the Boatman to take him across. Almost each time he feared the end of all, he remembered his God; the psychic came forward; the being was instantly illumined. God was not far from him or he was not far from his God. He could return easily to his psychic. That is not a mean spiritual achievement for a public figure. Let us listen to his aspiration:

> Before the end of my journey
> may I reach within myself

8. Sri Aurobindo, *SABCL*, vol. 18, pp. 33-34.

the one which is the All,
leaving the outer shell
to float away with the drifting multitude
upon the current of chance and change.[9]

Sri Aurobindo runs after God with an intense passion in *I Have a Hundred Lives,* a sonnet written early in his life. In his later sonnets, the passion leaves him making room for a higher emotion shaping itself out in experiential stuff. In most of Sri Aurobindo's sonnets, experience is recorded in a kind of action narrative, which is in sharp contrast with the leisurely emotion of Tagore. While Sri Aurobindo is in action, Tagore is dreaming about his beloved Lord in a leisurely manner:

I have ever loved thee in a hundred forms and times,
Age after age, in birth following birth.
The chain of songs that my fond heart did weave
Thou graciously didst take around thy neck,
Age after age, in birth following birth.

When I listen to the tales of the primitive past,
The love-pang of the far distant times,
The meetings and partings of the ancient ages,
I see thy form gathering light
Through the dark dimness of eternity
And appearing as a star ever fixed in the memory of the All.

We two have come floating by the twin currents of love
That well up from the inmost heart of the Beginningless.
We two have played in the lives of myriad lovers
In tearful solitude of sorrow,
In tremulous shyness of sweet union,
In old old love ever renewing its life.[10]

---

9. *The English Writings of Rabindranath Tagore,* New Delhi, Sahitya Akademi, 1994, vol. I, p. 476.

10. *The English Writings of Rabindranath Tagore,* vol. II, Sahitya Akademi, p. 328.

The talk of rebirth or many lives links him with Sri Aurobindo. Instead of the quick-flowing lines of Sri Aurobindo's sonnet, we have here a slow-moving dream of past lives. The phrase "chain of songs" is typically Tagorean, because he has always wished to seize the Divine through his songs. From birth to birth, the songs have formed a "chain of songs," a song sequence consisting in various tunes of joy and sadness. There is a leisurely nostalgia in lines 6 and 7, which speaks of Tagore's constant involvement in the love stories of medieval and ancient India. Let us have a look at Sri Aurobindo's sonnet:

> I have a hundred lives before me yet
> To grasp thee in, O Spirit ethereal,
> Be sure I will with heart insatiate
> Pursue thee like a hunter through them all.
> Thou yet shalt turn back on the eternal way
> And with awakened vision watch me come
> Smiling a little at errors past and lay
> Thy eager hand in mine, its proper home.
> Meanwhile made happy by thy happiness
> I shall approach thee in things and people dear,
> And in thy spirit's motions half-possess,
> Loving what thou hast loved, shall feel thee near,
> Until I lay my hands on thee indeed
> Somewhere among the stars, as "twas decreed."[11]

The sonnet has a suppressed glow of emotion in its action-oriented lines. Instead of the traditional nostalgia, we have here a memory of the future. Sri Aurobindo enjoys looking forward. Tagore's beautiful phrase "twin currents of love" is also applicable to Sri Aurobindo, who too knows that his love is a two-way traffic. There is a strong resolution to run after his beloved in the lives to come and to grasp him at last. His

---

11. Sri Aurobindo, *Sonnets*, Sri Aurobindo Ashram, Pondicherry, 1980, p. 83.

"insatiable" heart is throbbing with a white fire of love. The image of the hunter stresses the note of a one-pointed chase. God's hands are also keen on holding the human hands. The image of the "eternal way" is expressive of the quest of the human individual, who is here a hunter of Light. Who hunts whom? Both are hunters and the hunted. The human hand is God's proper home. The poet knows that even the very little things in Nature are God's favourites. Why not touch then the Lords's favourites before the great moment of union arrives? Both Tagore and Sri Aurobindo are certain about the response from the other side.

Any effort at refinement gives a touch of class to love poetry. The finer taste always moves beyond the immediate occasion, beyond the mundane and the familiar, seeking to reach an unseizable mystery. That is precisely the strength of Tagore, who is a love poet of the middle world. His lyrics are fairy tales with hidden symbols.

> There is a looker-on who sits behind my eyes. It seems he has seen things, in ages and worlds beyond memory's shore, and those forgotten sights glisten on the grass, and shiver on the leaves. He has seen under new veils the face of the one beloved, in twilight hours of many a nameless star. Therefore his sky seems to ache with the pain of countless meetings and paintings, and a longing pervades this spring breeze — the longing that is full of the whisper of ages without beginning.[12]

There is a prescient love in Tagore pressing him all the time. He enjoys the pain like a seeker of Light, but expresses it more as an aesthete than as a spiritual poet. He speaks repeatedly that he will meet one day the Life within him of

12. *The English Writings of Rabindranath Tagore,* vol. II, p. 208.

which he has only known in glimpses. Its fitful breath has come upon him from time to time making his thoughts fragrant for a while. A queer emotion gives birth to the following lines:

> I will meet one day the Joy without me that dwells behind the screen of light and will stand in the overflowing solitude where all things are seen by their creator.[13]

This is not exactly the voice of the Spirit, but a deliberate prescience of a future glory. That is why Nolini Kanto Gupta cautions us in his essay on *Mystic Poetry*: "To equate mysticism and spirituality is not always happy or even correct."[14] But then, who will deny the beauty and originality of Tagore's mystic love poetry? Sri Aurobindo, who has mapped the zones of human consciousness, is certainly the best judge of the nature of every emotion, mundane or divine. Standing at the summit of spirituality, he is able to see all the varieties of emotion, which lead to the supreme Godhead.

> Love comes to us in many ways; it may come as an awakening to the beauty of the Lover, by the sight of an ideal face and image of him; by his mysterious hints to us of himself behind the thousand faces of things in the world by a slow or sudden need of the heart; by a vague thirst in the soul; by the sense of someone near us drawing us or pursuing us with love or someone blissful or beautiful whom we must discover.[15]

The passage reads like an interpretation of Tagore's mystic love poetry. In fact, it may be used on the flap jacket of any edition of *Gitanjali*. Yet, the love lyrics of Tagore are quite different from Sri Aurobindo's own practice. Except for *The Dream Boat*, there is no trace of the Tagorean poetic style in Sri

---

13. Ibid., p. 164.
14. Nolini Kanto Gupta, *Collected Works*, vol. II, p. 64.
15. Sri Aurobindo, *SABCL*, vol. 21, *The Synthesis of Yoga*, p. 578.

Aurobindo. Even in *The Dream Boat,* the nature of agony is more Aurobindonian than Tagorean because of the control over the psychic sadness. In Tagore, the theme usually produces a kind of romantic anguish, as in Poem no. 16 in *Crossing.* There is another variety from Tagore in the following lines:

> In the NIGHT the song came to me; but you were not there. It found the words for which I had been seeking all day. Yes, in the stillness a moment after dark they throbbed into music, even as the stars then began to pulse with light; but you were not there. My hope was to sing it to you in the morning, but, try as I might, though the music came, the words hung back, when you were beside me.[16]

Sri Aurobindo's love lyrics are less popular than Tagore's because the experiences come from deeper layers of consciousness. All the mature sonnets are records of *yoga* put in that particular poetic form. If nobody has written about his life, he has done it himself in his lyrics and sonnets. They speak of another kind of love, which we can only guess.

> I who have felt the hungry heart of earth
> Aspiring beyond heaven to Krishna's feet.[17]

> He has become my substance and my breath;
> He is my anguish and my ecstasy.[18]

This is the characteristic intensity of Sri Aurobindo's emotion, which grows in further intensity in the speeches of *Savitri* in his cosmic epic. The poet's mind is settled on God. He loses himself in the deep ecstasy of his presence. The heart has become the radiantly unfolding lotus of the Spirit. Love has gone beyond the highest power of the normal human emotions.

---

16. *The English Writings of Rabindranath Tagore,* vol. I, p. 266.
17. Sri Aurobindo, *SABCL,* vol. 5, *Collected Poems,* p. 139.
18. Ibid., p. 152.

That is why Sri Aurobindo's love lyrics demand a special kind of audience.

Translation is not just a fraud. It may be absurd at times. The rhythm and vibrations are part and parcel of mantric poetry or the poetry of incantation. How could one translate Tagore's *aaji joto tara tobo akashe*? I was wondering about that, as I walked through the long procession of the singing crowd the night before the *Pous Mela*, that cold night of 22 December, which brings in the song freshly every year. It reminds us of the forgotten stars and the mighty face hidden behind them. We walk in the cool night through the tall dark trees and feel an ecstasy rising with the song, spreading everywhere its intense fragrance. The song seizes the Divine and pulls him down to the singing procession! Or He is trapped by Tagore's words. Nobody could translate the song. If it was mantric poetry, it was born for a particular language. However, there are lyrics by Tagore, — the poetry of prayer, love and pain — which may be perceived even in the translations. They may be studied with reference to certain poems by Sri Aurobindo.

Throughout his life, Tagore seems to have kept an eye on the Divine. It seems to have been a constant memory. And it seems to have kept him conscious all the time about the temple within, which is to be cleaned repeatedly for the smooth installation of the Presence there. His poetry speaks of this long rapport with a Presence playing hide and seek with him throughout his life. The painful theme of Sri Aurobindo's *The Dream Boat* is a recurring idea in Tagore's poetry. It is expressed in different ways and with different metaphors, not just in *Gitanjali*, but also in lyrics written after 1912. The failure of timing is an eternal spiritual crisis for the pilgrim soul. Let us listen to that crisis in poem no. 26 in *Gitanjali*:

> He came and sat by my side but I woke not. What a cursed sleep it was, O miserable me! He came when the night was still, he had his harp in his hands, and my dreams became resonant with its melodies. Alas, why are my nights all thus lost? Ah, why do I ever miss his sight whose breath touches my sleep?[19]

The same pain is expressed in a different way in *Crossing* (16):

> You came to my door in the dawn and sang; it angered me to be awakened from sleep, and you went away unheeded.
> You came in the noon and asked for water; it vexed me in my work, and you were sent away with reproaches.
> You came in the evening with your flaming torches,
> You seemed to me like a terror and I shut my door.
> Now in the midnight I sit alone in my lampless room and call you back whom I turned away in insult.[20]

Sri Aurobindo's *The Dream Boat* is a more realistic presentation of his spiritual tragedy caused by the failure of response. It lacks the colourful imagery of Tagore, but it is more painful than Tagore's mystic lyrics on response failure. In the first stanza, the soul listens to the query of the "gold god":

> Do you come now? is the heart's fire ready?[21]

Stanza two speaks of the response failure in a way, which is perfectly real to the spiritual pilgrim. The specific problem is contained in the two lines —

> It recalled all that the life's joy cherished,
> Imaged the felicity it must have lost for ever. . .[22]

This is specifically the reason why man refuses to say "yes" to

---

19. *The English Writings of Rabindranath Tagore*, vol. I, p. 50.
20. Ibid., p. 223.
21. Sri Aurobindo, *SABCL*, vol. 5, p. 561.
22. Ibid.

the infinite adventure. He is too fond of the earthly joys and fears to leave the charming things of our little life. The last stanza is exactly expressive of the tragic situation in the life of an individual. Sri Aurobindo chooses two simple words — "hollowness" and "void" — to indicate the result of a wrong choice.

> Now within the hollowness of the world's breast inhabits —
> For the love died and the old joy ended —
> Void of a felicity that has fled, gone for ever,
> And the gold god and the dream boat come not.[23]

In Tagore, the prayer for purification is quite genuine. This poetry puts on a new colour in the English translation made by the poet himself:

> Do not turn away thy face from my
> heart's dark secrets, but burn them
> till they are alight with thy fire.[24]

And here is a translation by Aurobindo Bose:

> Touch me with thy fire,
> Burn and purify my life,
> Lift my body
> And make it thy temple lamp.
> Let my songs be the oil
> That feeds the flame.
> In the core of Darkness
> Stars blossom forth at thy touch,
> And my agony aflame
> Rises to heaven.[25]

---

23. Ibid.

24. *The English Writings of Rabindranath Tagore,* vol. I, p. 220.

25. Aurobindo Bose (tr.). *Later Poems of Tagore with a foreword by Yehudi Menuhin,* New Delhi, Orient Paperbacks, 1978. p. 84.

Like Sri Aurobindo, Tagore knows well that pain is the hammer of God and that God is an oppressor because He loves. *Crossing*: 6 is an obvious echo of Sri Aurobindo's philosophy of the mystery of suffering.

> Thou hast done well, my lover, thou hast done well to send
> me thy fire of pain.
> For my incense never yields its perfume till it burns and my
> lamp is blind till it is lighted.
> When my mind is numb its torpor must be stricken
> by thy love's lightning;
> And the very darkness that blots my world burns like a torch
> when set afire by thy thunder.[26]
> Have you come to me as my sorrow? All the more I must
> cling to you.
> Your face is veiled in the dark, all the more I must see you.
> At the blow of death from your hand let my life leap up
> in a flame.
> Tears flow from my eyes — let them flow round your feet in
> worship.
> And let the pain in my breast speak to me that you are still
> mine.[27]

For Sri Aurobindo, pain means this and also something different. He is a deputy of the aspiring world and his is a god's labour, which is to lift man to God and also to bring God down to man:

> I have laboured and suffered in Matter's night
> To bring the fire to man;
> But the hate of hell and human spite
> Are my need since the world began.[28]

In Tagore's poetry the psychic comes out frequently in various forms, but most interestingly in the love lyrics:

---

26. *The English Writings of Rabindranath Tagore,* vol. I, p. 220.
27. Ibid., p. 225.
28. Sri Aurobindo, *SABCL,* vol. 5, p. 99.

> You will lead me from star to star to waken me in new mornings of love. It is your love that draws out the flow of my being through the maze of channels of new life over your endless worlds.
>
> You will startle me with new visions of fulfilment at every bend of the road and fashion my moments with immortal forms of joy.[29]

Early in his life, Sri Aurobindo expresses his love for the Divine in this simple way in his sonnet entitled *I Have A Hundred Lives,* which we have quoted earlier in this chapter. In Sri Aurobindo's lyrics, we rarely see the gesture of prayer. He speaks of his experiences of love and pain and those feelings are too far from us. That is precisely the reason why Sri Aurobindo has failed to become a popular lyric poet. This surely is not to degrade the status of Tagore, the lyricist, who is the first among the modern Bengali poets to use the lyric as a means of ascension of consciousness.

29. *The English Writings of Rabindranath Tagore,* vol. I, p. 337.

7

Rabindra Sangeet
The Songs of Tagore

TAGORE began writing songs at about age of 13. When he wrote the song *Jwal Jwal Chita* for Jyotirindranath's play *Sarojini,* he was 14.[1] It went on ceaselessly as a life-long search for ecstasy in various things, mundane and spiritual. He wrote about 2,500 songs. He began developing his theory of music quite early in his life. His essay on "Music and Poetry" (*Sangeet O Kabita*) came out in 1882, when he was barely 21. Only a year before, his two musical plays *Balmiki Protibha* and *Kaalmrigoya* had been published. His essays on music are rare as compared to his articles on poetry and other arts. But then, he took up the issue quite frequently in his letters and discussions, diaries and memoirs and at other places in passing. In fact, he lived continuously with music.

Time may fade the image of the poet, but it will be hard for it to stifle the voice of Tagore, the musician and the creator of *Rabindra Sangeet,* which is an unforgettable glory of the romantic spirit in man. Tagore was not a champion of Indian classical music, although he had an intimate knowledge of its grammar. He revived the spirit of Indian classical music in his own queer ways, the ways of a romantic and a creative

1. Satyendranath Roy (ed.), *Rabindranather Chintajagat*: *Shilpo Chinta*: *Rabindra Rachona Sankolan,* Granthaloy Private Limited, Kolkata, 1996, p. 48.

composer. He drew inspiration from the other sources of Indian music, like the folk songs, the *kirtan*s and other religious songs, *kabigaan, brohmo sangeet* (initiated by Rammohun Roy), patriotic songs, songs for stage plays and *yatra* (melodramatic theatre), *panchali, tarja, akhraai, toppa* and the like. He was also inspired by some Western tunes. As a revolutionary composer, he broke away from the expressive modes of Indian classical music in his search for a new form of expression based on the marriage between words and tunes. This fusion created a new art. The musical value of the composers of Bollywood in the 1050s and 1960s cannot be estimated properly without an understanding of Tagore's achievement as a musician. If Tagore is the first modern composer in the field of Indian music, the post-moderns are men like Naushad and Roshan and Madan Mohan, who created the classics for a new age with the help of poets like Shakeel Badayuni, Sahir Ludhianvi, Kaifi Azmi and others.

The purists were not quite kind to Tagore's music. They hit back. It pricked the sensitive skin of a poet. He defended boldly, often ironically. In the May-June issue of *Bharati* in 1881, he wrote:

> Am I bribed by *Jay Jawanti,* that I'll have to sacrifice my life for it? It is distressing for any sensitive listener, when he sees the *ustād*s of today sweating heavily and making terrible faces while singing and thereby shifting the sense behind the song. . . . The different *sur*s needed for different *rāga*s had been fixed up long before. I don't feel any need to work hard on them. Now, music will really be benefited if the purists concentrate on trying to discover the different ideas behind those *rāga*s.[2]

---

2. Ibid., p. 305.

The sense behind an Indian *raga* or *ragini* is the thing which matters most for Tagore. Why does *Purbi* remind us of the evening? And why does *Bhairon* bring in the memory of dawn? Both abound in the soft *surs*. Then why do they produce different moods? In *Bhairon,* the *sur* must expand and rise slowly; in *Purbi,* the *sur* passes away slowly like the fading away of a sweet soft murmur. The dawn opens the eyes slowly; the night closes the eyes gently. There lies the similarity. Tagore wished to discover the words through the *surs*. But he did not always stick to that principle. He could not. For situations needed other methods of composition. In 1921, in an interview with Marguerite Wilkinson, he said:

> Sometimes I make the words first and then put music to them later. Sometimes I make a melody first and then put words to it. Sometimes the music is subordinated to the words. Sometimes, the words are subordinated to the music.[3]

The best composition forms a total harmony between the words and tunes. One cannot separate them. The purpose is to create a *third art,* which is neither poetry nor *sur.* Poetry and *sur* consent to give birth to a third existence that is true *Rabindra Sangeet.* A very ordinary poem may be transformed into a bright creation with the addition of *sur.* In an interview with Edward Thompson in 1926, Tagore drew our notice to his sense of tradition and creativity:

> In my hymns, my *Brohmosangit,* I have adapted and taken wholesale older tunes from Tansen, the best of our composers; in these, I have used orthodox forms. But for my own songs I have invented freely.[4]

Like the Mother and Sri Aurobindo, Tagore insists on the soul value of music. The psychic touch is more important than

3. Ibid., p. 347.
4. Ibid., p. 364.

a demonstration of grammar, which is quite often mere pedanticism. He prefers *kirtan* to the dry exhibition of the grammarian. He does not use the word psychic; he struggles to mean it in a letter to Dilip Kumar Roy written on July 29, 1937.[5] In that letter we find him insisting on a Bengalee voice for *kirtan,* because according to him the form demands a special mellow sensitivity, a depth of sense, which goes away with the harsh presentation of a classical vocalist. On 29 October 1937, he says, in a letter to Dilip Kumar Roy, that nobody can resist the union of words and *sur.* "They want each other."[6] In his letter to Dilip Kumar Roy written on 6 February 1938, Tagore claims originality in a humorous address to Tansen. "Ustadji, my path is also yours."[7] It is the path of new creation.

Tagore missed Sahana Devi, who had sacrificed her musical ambition in favour of her love for the Mother and Sri Aurobindo. He missed her because she could open the inmost being while singing and there was no stylization in her presentation. On 4 April 1938, he wrote to Sahana Devi clarifying his interest in her renderings:

> When you sing my songs, I feel my compositions have become meaningful. In that rendering I'm there as much as you are there. . . .[8]

Tagore was possibly meaning Sahana's capacity to realize the soul-value of his words. The proper rendering of the inspiration must be there. The Mother rightly observes:

> But what I mean is that there is an inner condition in which the external form is not the most important thing; it is the origin of the music, the inspiration from beyond, which is

5. Ibid., p. 403.
6. Ibid., p. 404.
7. Ibid., p. 406.
8. Ibid., p. 407.

> important; it is not purely the sounds, it is what the sounds express.[9]

Although it is not possible to translate the spiritual or the mystic atmosphere of the Bengali songs, a few samples may be cited to introduce the themes of some lyrics to the non-Bengali readers. These samples will tell why Tagore is a gateway to the words of the Mother and Sri Aurobindo and why Sri Aurobindo has seen a great possibility in music.

> Art, poetry, music, as they are in their ordinary functioning, create mental and vital, not spiritual values; but they can be turned to a higher end, and then, like all things that are capable of linking our consciousness to the Divine, they are transmuted and become spiritual and can be admitted as part of a life of *yoga.* All takes new values not from itself, but from the consciousness that uses it; for there is only one thing essential, needful, indispensable, to grow conscious of the Divine Reality and live in it and live it always.[10]

One must say that the effort is always there in Tagore. His aspiration takes beautiful shapes: beautiful flowers, fragrance in the air, prayer for purity and Grace, the sound of the Divine's flute and so many things revealing the soul's ultimate choice!

> With the light of mine eyes I saw the outside:
> Now when the light is gone, I see the self within.
> In the playhouse of the world I had played with thee —
> Let that play be over and the meeting of hearts begin,
> The string of the *vina* has snapped,
> The *vina* of the heart now sings.[11]

---

9. *On Music: Words of Sri Aurobindo and the Mother,* Sri Aurobindo Society Pondicherry, p. 5.

10. Ibid., pp. 37-38.

11. Aurobindo Bose, Trans. With a Foreword by Yehudi Menuhin, *Poems of Tagore,* Orient Paperbacks, p. 84.

The translator, a Bengalee, has drifted away a bit from the original. And yet one can easily feel Tagore's efforts at self-purification through music. Sudhir Chakraborty, in his article entitled *Nirjan Ekoker Gaan*[12] (*The Song of a Loner Sung to Himself*) has indicated the spiritual aspiration of Tagore, which is very prominent due to his choice of the *raga Bhairobi* between the years 1892 and 1939. Chakraborty draws our attention to the psychic sadness of *Bhairobi* expressed through the songs "The Flute knows my true word" (1915), "The song that plays in my being" (1921), "I don't know to whom I sing my songs" (1939), "Days pass by" (1926), "Why are my eyes flooding with tears, (1892) and many others, which speak of a loner's painful quest. Unlike European music, which is mostly addressed to humanity, Tagore's music is singularly individual. Sankho Ghosh has seen the same aspiration in Tagore's songs.

> Tagore's songs are there to build him up from inside. It is a ceaseless music of self-awareness and self-teaching. In this pedestal of self-teaching, I examine my daily life. I see that no lotus has bloomed in my heart centre. Alas! Beauty won't choose to implant Her feet there. This sense of waste, incapacity and incompleteness makes him weep.[13]

While this quest for self-knowledge is obsessive in the songs of the *puja* phase in *Gitobitan,* Tagore goes out to the world of Nature too. He feels the Divine in trees and flowers, in streams and seas, in the green and the bareness, and in the nights too, when he looks up to discover bright flames burning in the stars.

---

12. See *Rabindra Smarak Grantha*: *Probondho Sankolon,* Visva-Bharati, 1991, pp. 148-49.

13. Sankho Ghose, *E Amir Aboron,* pp. 21-22, translated by the author.

He composed songs for every season in Bengal. When rains set in, he was specially thrilled. Then it was not just aesthetics. The rains brought in old memories in a new world; the jingling sound took his heart away. He struggled to remember who had come in the nights to call him. He saw a shadow in his dream and wondered: Who had come? The next chapter contains some efforts at translation.

8

Songs of Tagore and the Great Singers

How important are the songs as poetry? Are they very fine lyrics when the tunes or *sur* are not set to them? The collection entitled *Gitobitan*[1] shows that most of the songs have immense poetic value. They are compressed and their economy of expression speaks of the class of Tagore as a lyric poet. They are strangely beautiful lyrics. Religion verges on spirituality; the mystic sense spreads out in different directions; love is mellow and refined with all the foresight of things to come, the prescient memory of the Supernature leaning on our small lives.

He hopes that his silent moments will become full with the Divine's music. At the end of the day, when it is dark, stars of music will show up in millions. One day his emptied flute will ring out. He prays for silence again and again to listen to the flute of the Divine. He wishes all his words to float away so that he may be able to enjoy the music of silence. Nights are soothing and intensely silent in song no. 256. Tagore speaks here about the poetry of incantation in the line *nirob mantre hridoy majhe shanti shanti baaje. . . .*

---

1. Rabindranath Tagore, *Gitobitan,* 1931, Kolkata, Visva-Bharati.

Peace, peace and peace
That is the *mantra* whispered in silence
Inside my heart.[2]

The element of wonder is quite often coloured by the psychic. The poet wonders how the Lord sings. He pines for expression, which will echo that ethereal song. He broods over his incapacity. He could not see the presence inside him. The vital obstructed his sight. And the psychic wept. Song no. 139 speaks of an authentic sadness pushed forward by the inmost being:

If I do not meet you, my Lord, in this life,
then let me remember that I didn't get you
in the last life.
Let me not forget,
let me feel the pain then
in sleep as in waking.

Time floats away in vital cravings. All is lost in this life of indiscipline. An unusual call to the World Mother enters into song no. 160. Mother-worship is rare in Tagore, but who can ignore the spell of the charmed name? The poet prays to her for a supreme inwardization. The psychic sadness is frequent in the poet who is caught between the two worlds. Why is it that I catch a glimpse of you only from time to time? Why not forever? Why are the clouds obstructing my sight? Where can I find that great love to trap you forever? These are moments of real pain and only the earth-bound soul having an eye for heaven knows the reality behind Tagore's psychic sadness. All the pilgrims pass by and time too. Where lies the light beyond the seas? In song no. 426, the dark night of the soul is obvious and yet that Tagorean or Aurobindonian optimism is the final note. One day the deep dark shall be changed to an intense delight with the sound of the *veena* of the All-Delight.

2. Except for the translations made by Tagore for the English *Gitanjali*, all other translations in the essay are by the author.

The winds of spring shall bring in the Lord's frankincense into the centre of the poet's heart.

The full impact of the psychic is rare in world literature, as Sri Aurobindo tells Sethna in a letter:

> The psychic being usually expresses itself through its instruments, mental, vital and physical; it tries to put as much of its own stamp on them as possible. But it can seldom put on them the full psychic stamp . . . it comes fully out from its rather secluded and overshadowed position and takes into its hands the direct government of the nature.[3]

Yet the little of his best self that Tagore applies to his songs has given them a rare glory. He addresses the Divine softly to remind Him of the songs he had sung for Him and the songs He had sung to him. In the rainy nights and in the fragrant air of the spring memories will never cease to come. There were sports at one time with the Divine without the knowledge of His identity. There was no fear, no shame in those spontaneous moments. Life moved on restlessly. There were calls from Him, repeated calls, in the dawns, as if they were calls from his best friend. The poet smiled and ran with Him in the forests and beyond them into the far away lands. Alas! who knew the meaning of His songs then? Only his restless heart sang and danced with His songs. It was a strange blend of the psychic and the finer vital. Now a sudden moment of the soul sees what was never seen before:

> What image do we see at the end of the game?
> The sky stands still, the sun and the moon are quiet,
> the universe stands still
> with his eyes down on your feet![4]

---

3. *Overhead Poetry*, 1972, ed. K.D. Sethna, p. 7.
4. *Gitanjali*, 64.

Between despair and psychic sadness, the psychic prayers creep in frequently indicating the aspiration in the past. He wishes his love to move always towards the Divine. Quite often he feels that this life is a failure and that only grace can bring in a miraculous success. He wishes the eternal songs of the Divine to ring in his ears all the time, in the night as in the day. Time and again, we find Tagore brooding over distractions and the loss of time. Fear rises in his heart quite frequently — the fear of the quickly moving time, the fear of the sun going down, the fear of the darkness enveloping the earth, the fear of the capsizing boat. Where lies the Ocean? How far is it? Without the Divine, everything is painful. Nothing counts but that just a small place on the soil under His feet! He wishes to be the last in the procession of pilgrims, to occupy the last seat. But he needs a place by His Grace. Sometimes there is an intense prayer to keep his head down on His feet, as we see in that famous *Gitanjali* poem, which is poem no. 492 in *Gitobitan.* The great Aurobindonian caution rings out in the poem: let me not glorify myself by using Your name and nothing but Your wish be my wish. There are such moments of high living in Tagore's *Gitobitan.*

Quite a few songs echo the theme of Sri Aurobindo's *The Dream Boat.* Poem no. 8 in *Gitobitan* speaks of this call coming from a boat, in times of thunder and tempest, in the rainy nights of July, the call for death. The poet looks at the boatman and keeps sitting on the shore. In song no. 102, the poet prays to the Lord to stay close to him, even when he is not responsive and to wake him up with a painful stroke. In song no. 403, the poet has realized that those whom he had chosen instead of God are no more responsive to him. They came and left him alone in the desert. Transient smiles pass by and the lamps go out in the dark. Who remains then to wipe away his tears? He sees none around. The sun and the moon and the stars are lost. And the Lord does not come. One instantly remembers the last lines of Sri Aurobindo's *The Dream Boat,* where we see a very sad image of emptiness and void.[5]

In quite a few songs, Tagore's theory of surplus is seen in practice. Things come to the poet more than he needs, more than the frame requires. The mud wall of the self is flooded. Tagore's boat is not just an ordinary boat; it is a singing boat floating towards the edge of the Infinite. Sometimes, he is painfully aware of the incapacity of his songs. It is then that he invites the Lord to sing or to play on the flute. The incapacity of his songs gives birth to some remarkable lyrics. The effective song is elusive. But, the wish to sing is too intense. Let me use Tagore's own translation here from the English *Gitanjali*:

> I am here to sing thee songs. In this hall of thine I have
> a corner seat.
> In thy world I have no work to do; my useless life can
> only break out in tunes without a purpose.
> When the hour strikes for thy silent worship at the dark
> temple of midnight, command me, my master, to stand
> before thee to sing.
> When in the morning air the golden harp is tuned,
> honour me, commanding my presence.[6]

Sad to say, this was one of the miserable failures of translation. However, the importance of song in his life is unmistakable even in this poor translation. The search for the true song continues. In song no. 24 in *Gitobitan,* the poet prepares a seat by the road with the help of his songs. He addresses the Lord as a "pilgrim" and invites Him to take a seat by him again and again. The shadow of the clouds falls on the forest; in the

---

5. Sri Aurobindo, *SABCL,* vol. 5, p. 561.
6. *Gitanjali,* 15.

corner of the blue eyes of the sky water is taking shape. Today, the Lord comes in a new dress to the forests of palm trees at the end of the meadow. The poet urges him not to pass by secretly; he urges him to stay in the cloudy dark of his rain-songs. The game of songs is a leisurely game, which has no material benefit. But, the immaterial is immensely valuable to the poet. The pilgrim soul is a singer. He waits with his basket of songs outside the Great Palace. Who knows which song will touch his heart? The search for the true song is the search for the poetry of incantation. Poetry goes on searching for the word beyond words. Poetry is song. It is a passion to utter the mantric word, which is immense joy. Footsteps come closer and then they move away. Song no. 13 in *Gitanjali* is a better translation, if we keep in mind the fact that English is a masculine language:

> The song that I came to sing remains unsung to this day.
> I have spent my days in stringing and in unstringing my instrument.
> The time has not come true, the words have not been rightly set; only
> there is the agony of wishing in my heart.
> The blossom has not opened; only the wind is singing by.
> I have not seen his face, nor have I listened to his voice;
> only I have heard his gentle footsteps from the road before my house.
> The livelong day has passed in spreading his seat
> on the floor; but the lamp has not been lit and I cannot ask
> him into my house. I live in the hope of meeting with him;
> but this meeting is not yet.[7]

Tagore's shorter units are obviously more effective than the longer lyrics, which sometimes aim at an epic style and fail

---

7. Ibid., 13.

miserably, simply because his genius is far from the Epic. It is in the shorter lyrics, especially meant to be sung, that he appears to us as a remarkable genius. Call him a butterfly or a chameleon, he is a strange angel tasting the multiple varieties of the great Essence and expressing his delight and pain as a taster. He is never out of touch; he is charmed by the sights and smells spread around him; he is never tired of his search for the keys through his songs. In song no. 46 of the *Worship* phase in *Gitobitan,* he is aspiring for an Aurobindonian calm and blending, that slowed-down gesture with the emotional mood of Chandidasa. Let me try a translation:

> Slow my Friend, very slowly
> let me walk up to your lonely temple.
> I don't know the way,
> there is not a drop of light anywhere,
> it is dark replacing dark
> inside out,
> I've just received
> the sound of your footsteps
> in this dense forest.
>
> Slow my Friend, very slowly
> let me walk alongside the edge of the dark.
> I'll walk in the night
> following the signal of your breeze,
> I've received today
> the smell of your clothes
> in this breeze of the Spring.[8]

Sri Aurobindo would have called it half-thought. The deeper sense is obvious. There is a genuine memory of our true being that pines for the far-away smell, which pierces open the mud wall of our self from time to time. For Tagore, it becomes an

8. Rabindranath Tagore, *Gitanjali,* 1979, Kolkata, Visva-Bharati Granthan Bibhag, p. 25, translated from Bengali by the author.

unavoidable call quite often, so acute that only in songs he hopes to find some relief, some release from the bondage of his little self. One drop of lyric relaxes his tension of death, desire and incapacity. He wakes up to listen to that invitation to go far, beyond the seas into a secret continent. He wakes up with an attitude of response, telling the caller that he has cast aside the burden, that he wishes to be taken ahead with him and that he wishes to feel the soothing breeze of the silent night to quench his thirst. All his words will float away with the tune of the caller.

In a song running to eighteen lines (*Worship* no. 59, *Gitobitan*), Tagore's perception of motiveless love is in line with the grand principle of love expressed by Sri Aurobindo in *The Synthesis of Yoga*:

> I wish to offer you something
> even if you don't need it.
> When I saw you,
> you were roaming about
> alone in the lonely dense forest
> in the dark.
> Then I wished to lit a lamp
> on your path,
> even if you didn't need it.[9]

Those who deny the word "spiritual" to Tagore, must consider the approving words of Sri Aurobindo on the finer emotional motives of even the common man, who rises above the common in those rare moments of consciousness.

> It is so that life can be changed into worship — by putting behind it the spirit of a transcendent and universal love, the seeking of oneness, the sense of oneness; by making each act a symbol, an expression of Godward emotion or a

9. Ibid., p. 30, translated by the author.

> relation with the Divine; by turning all we do into an act of worship, an act of the soul's communion, the mind's understanding, the life's obedience, the heart's surrender.[10]

Tagore's songs thus become a symbol, an expression and a positive step taken towards the God-province. Each song in the *Worship* phase in *Gitobitan* is an example of sincerity, but there are some which are just smells of a sacred incense. Everything is taken; nothing is refused. Rabindra Sangeet is sacred action, and the confirmation of such works is very clear in the *Gita.* The song is synonymous with the examples of a leaf, a flower, a fruit or a cup of water, in fact anything which is offered with devotion. It is something more, a very precious gift of love, a gift which has come from the Divine, who wishes to get back the same thing from the human individual. Receiving the song from the Lord, Tagore returns that as a gift of love. It is a strange love-game, taking and returning. This alone will prove why Sri Aurobindo found in Tagore a wayfarer to the Divine. Tagore's song is an action done under the spell of Godward emotion. Even when he diverges in the Nature-lyrics, the love lyrics and the lyrics on various other themes, he can always come back through his own queer ways or he can achieve a refined aesthetics creating his own religion. Tagore's very inspiration and respiration, his very heartbeats, are made conscious in him as the living rhythm of the universal love.

There are songs, which have grown out of the dark night of the soul. That too confirms the pilgrim march. There are frequent broodings over persistent spells of darkness. He wriggles as if in a cave of darkness. Darkness leads to further darkness. Obstacles stay for a long time. When will it cease to burn? When will this darkness be filled up with delight? When

10. Sri Aurobindo, *SABCL,* vol. 20, *The Synthesis of Yoga*, p. 153.

will the flute of the All-Delight light up my soul? Well, let darkness be there encircling me, but let the great touch keep me awake in the midst of gloom. This gesture shapes itself out in different songs.

Oblivion is pain. He sings of rests and distractions. But they are temporary failures for him. Once he has known the goal, he never loses its memory, the memory of a glorious future. He sees kindness in the apparent cruelty of the Divine. Who can receive the Great Light without preparing for it? The jar of the mouth must expand by the heat of suffering, and it is only then that the divine's love may descend smoothly into the jar. Tagore seems to have known this Vedic concept of suffering. The Divine says "no," because He loves to say "yes" at the right moment and because the jar of the mouth or the human body needs to expand to receive the divine juice. A pre-mature consent will break the jar or the human body.

Too short lyrics lack the genuine fire of aspiration even when the tunes are set to them. Quite often, they are just musical exercises. They are minor poems by a great poet-singer, who just experiments with some Indian ragas. Tagore usually takes seven or eight lines to write a good poem as a song. Songs running to four or five lines are mostly dry poetry. They fail to image the sense of beyonding without the tunes.

And what about those great singers, who made the lyrics more expressive? They were interpreters. They were taught to sing, not to interpret. It was a choice of their creative spirits, the choice of the inmost being. They interpreted instinctively. They were perhaps asked to feel and mean the word. They did.

That made them discover the secret vibrations of the inmost self, which give a rare status to Art. Inspiration has its ways — queer ways. It made them suspend the intellectual mind, to see only and sing. It made them simple and natural. Even the Nature-songs sung by Santidev Ghosh indicates effort to tap the deeper emotional centres. There are times when Santidev is able to reach the deepest self with the utmost simplicity of a child. Greater still in his effort to interpret the incantatory verse of Tagore. In such moments, the moonlit even-fall and the smell of *Rajanigandha* take our longing souls beyond the ocean of Beauty in search of a far-away bliss. When we appreciate today's Swapna Ghosal or Swastika Mukherjee we appreciate their efforts to revive the spirit of Rabindra Sangeet, the free natural spirit, the simplicity and the quest for the soul-value of the mantric word. The technique of inspired art eludes the eye of the intellect. The inspired efflux shapes out its own technique. I refer to this because there are people who find fault with Sahana Devi's technique. To appreciate Sahana Devi requires a different kind of sensitivity, an ear of the soul.

The best Indian songs are rarely high poetry. Quite often the poetry is mediocre and the *sur* is not the best manifestation of a *Behag* or a *Kedar* or a *Kamod.* The words and the tune seek to marry in the right spirit and therefore each of them seeks to sacrifice. Out of this sacrifice, a new art is born. This new art — neither the tune nor the poetry — is totally independent, a new product. It is a *third art* born through the sacrifice made by the *sur* and the words. Rabindranath Tagore far outshines others in this field. Atulprosad Sen is another master. But, he works within a limited field.

Initiated listeners of Indian music will remember the popular songs of the 1950s and the 1960s created by the combined efforts of lyricists and composers — Naushad-Shakeel, Sahir-Ravi, Roshan-Mazrooh, Madan Mohan and Raja Mehdi Ali Khan — which shine bright still escaping the dust of time. There also one sees that marriage, that mutual sacrifice of words and tune. Unlike Naushad and Sahir, Tagore could handle his words and tune independently in his search for the *third art*. Naushad and Shakeel were co-creators of the *third art*.

Female singers have usually been more expressive than male singers. The reason is simple. Women can open the psychic more naturally than men. Dilip Kumar Roy knew the secret. He practised what he preached. A singer sings only when his soul sings. That was his belief. It seems natural, because Roy was an Aurobindonian. Unfortunately he was not a singer of Tagore songs. The Calcuttans will never forgive me for excluding Debobroto Biswas from my list of "greats". I appreciate his voice, not his expression. He suffered from melodrama and moved far away from the psychic, our true emotional centre. Notice the restraint of Suchitra Mitra when she sings *purāno janiā cheonā* and the lack of that when Debobroto handles the same song. Suchitra's problem lies in her strong intellectual sense. The intellectual mind is too predominant in the later Suchitra, which obstructs her true emotional fire. Her strong point is her technique; her weakness is also there. Yet Suchitra remains a great singer by virtue of her earlier efforts, where she uses her emotion remarkably in songs like *toomi kon bhāngoner pathe ele* or *ekodā toomi priye* or *deyā neyā phiriye deyā*. The early Suchitra Mitra is a remarkable blend of power and sweetness in songs like *āji godhuli lagone* and *bhebechhilem āsbe phire.*

Subinoy Roy, the best male singer of Tagore songs, is as technically perfect as Suchitra. He expresses the quiet and the serene with remarkable effect. Sweetness, discipline, pain, peace — Subinoy Roy combines many virtues. Yet he could have been a greater singer if he preferred the simple magic of the inmost being over his stress on the "aesthetics," which is certainly a high virtue below the "highest." The songs were given a new dimension by the great female singers like Sahana Devi, Rajeswari (Vasudeb) Dutta, Malati Ghosal, Kanika Banerji, Renuka Dasgupta, Kanak Das, Nilima Sen, Savitri Krishnan, and a few others.

What was common in them? All of them were great naturals. Purists will find a slip here or a jarring note there. But then, nothing can obscure their controlled emotional glow. The luminous leaves the veil behind and comes out straight through their songs. Was Kanika conscious of that play when she sang *āmi rūpe tomāy bholābo nā*? Did Rajeswari really try to find out the source, which coloured her vital despair in *āji je rajanī jāy*? One never really knows. But the thing is there, very authentic stamp of our veiled identity. Even Tagore, an aesthete, couldn't have hoped so much.

The more one thinks of Sahana Devi, the more one becomes conscious of the true attitude to a song. I heard her sing when she was 90. The song floated out of her room, moved out into the sea and then went straight up to woo the high far blue. Gasping for breath in her large room, that frail figure left a different message for me that afternoon in Pondicherry. She did not need to make gestures or acrobatics with an imported microphone in her hands. There was one language there — the language of the soul. Sri Aurobindo knew it as "the soul of the emotion."[11]

The psychic has hidden its face because of the tension of professionalism. The other obstacle to true music is the chaotic use of instruments and the noise produced by that electronic mishmash. Tagore-songs are basically noiseless songs. Their

---

11. Sri Aurobindo, *SABCL*, vol. 9, p. 15.

magic lies in their noiseless sweetness. The computer is welcome, but not computerized music. For, the computer is an important instrument to measure "Consciousness." We need the old flute, the old violin and the old *esraj* to do that. Let us return to that noiseless sweetness in the field of music. Noiselessness! how sweet is the word! That alone characterizes the achievement of a Malati Ghosal or a Sahana Devi or a Santosh Sengupta. The singers today are like loud competitive microphones in *puja pandal*s struggling hard to raise their voices so that we may identify them. Alas! we do not know them. Only the noise reaches us.

9

Gitanjali : The New Language and the New Spirituality

ALL creativity seeks a new language in the context of a native tradition. That is precisely the reason why we see modern critics of language, like Randolph Quirk and Donald J. Lloyd, defending the divergence of usage in Standard English. Lloyd was extremely catholic even in the mid-1950s: "We need not raise our eyebrows at a different twist of phrase, but enjoy it as an echo of a way of life somewhat different from our own . . . we need more exact and expressive mode of utterance than we have; we are working toward finer tolerances."[1] Today we have quite a few acceptable varieties: Indian English, Australian English, West Indian English, African English and the like.

An Indian writing like Shakespeare and Lawrence cannot hope to be creative. The true Indian can never think out or dream in a foreign atmosphere. When we do that, we cease to be creative. In 1912, Tagore was aware of it. Sri Aurobindo's appraisal of *Gitanjali* points to the reason of its success as a creative Indo-Anglian experiment.[2] Sri Aurobindo had known it earlier; his poetry written between 1890 and 1910 confirms

---

1. Mody C. Boatright & Leo Hughes, eds., *College Prose,* Boston, Houghton Miffin Company, 1956, p. 325.
2. Sri Aurobindo, *SABCL,* vol. 9, p. 453.

our belief. However, English was like his mother tongue and he could not afford to ignore the basic rhythms and patterns of the English language. He was thinking of harmonizing his feeling for his motherland with his impeccable sense of the English syntax and idiom. Here is an example from *Envoi*:

> Me from her lotus heaven Saraswati
> Has called to regions of eternal snow
> And Ganges pacing to the southern sea,
> Ganges upon whose shores the flowers of Eden blow.[3]

These oft-quoted lines speak of a creative experiment, a commitment to the motherland caught in the spontaneous lines of a maturing poet. Tagore's uncertain grasp of the language did not stand as an obstacle to the discovery of a new poetic language, which was neither purely English nor purely Bengali. It was a queer fusion of the two, which Yeats and Owen could realise easily and which an average Bengali with his/her little knowledge of the foreign language could feel intimately. It was a miraculous birth of a new poetic language, which Tagore could never repeat. The success of *Gitanjali* made him adventurous as a transcreator. It was a sad spectacle except for some brief glories here and there.

What Yeats calls "courtesy"[4] is actually a mellow Bengali sensitivity, which the Bengali race owes to Tagore. It is difficult to know how it shapes out in Tagore. The devotional poems of Bengal, the *Vaisnava Padavali* in particular, and a constant psychic influence on things vital could be the possible sources. It was an excessive surplus, an uncontrollable surplus. Even the angels fail to know why the eyes are flooded with tears, why on earth something swells up from the deep insides and

---

3. Sri Aurobindo, *SABCL*, vol. 5, p. 28.
4. Sisir Kumar Das, ed., *The English Writings of Rabindranath Tagore*, vol. I, New Delhi, Sahitya Akademi, 1994, p. 42.

chokes our throat! Yet one angel of surplus responds to the call from another, as Yeats does.

> I have carried the manuscript of these translations about with me for days, reading it in railway trains, or on the top of omnibuses and in restaurants and I have often had to close it lest some stranger would see how much it moved me.[5]

The "surplus" in man goes beyond his physical needs. It is an excess material indicating the liberation of the individual from the bondage of utility. When utility expires, man is invaded by the Infinite. This surplus is mirrored in the poems of *Gitanjali*. It is just another projection of the flame of aspiration, a kind of rejection of religion in favour of a purer love, which seems to be the only religion in poet's life. It is Radha's quest; it is that in terms of aesthetics:

> That I want thee, only thee — let my heart repeat without end. All desires that distract me, day and night, are false and empty to the core.[6]

When he is distracted from the far-away Infinite, Tagore searches for mundane ways, simple daily symbols of eternity, to keep the link. The finite flares up in the light of the Infinite: the flowers, the lights and the darkened earth, the clouds and the stars, the horizon and the sky, the bird and the river, the boat and the boatman, the way and the wayfarer.

The new spirituality is new by virtue of its integral approach to life and *yoga*, which accepts man's individual tastes and temperament in a material set up. The new *yogin* does not turn his face from the varied tastes of life, the common slides

5. Ibid., p. 39.
6. Ibid., p. 54.

of Nature, human joys and sufferings, the bombs in Tokyo and Barcelona and Afghanistan, games and sports. The evolving planet in the age of computer has left no place for the ascetic. The *rishi*s will be back in jeans and polyester. The spirituality opened up by Sri Ramakrishna and Sri Aurobindo does not see the Divine as a fearful object. He is a friend, a lover, a guide who never fails. But then, the new spirituality is also *sadhana* of simplicity, the rejection of luxury in this beautiful earth of science and materialism, a quest for the only love, the truly responsive love. Tagore's *Gitanjali* is a straight and simple introduction to this new approach to the Divine. The Bengali poet is certainly under the spell of *Vaisnava Padavali*, but somehow he has also accommodated the old Hebrew poets, the American Transcendentalists like Thoreau and Emerson, even Shelley and George Russell (A.E.), in *Gitanjali*. If it is not new spirituality in all its aspects, it is certainly new mysticism with its borderline lights.

> Ah, the light dances, my darling, at the centre of my life; the light strikes, my darling, the chords of my love; the sky opens, the wind runs wild, laughter passes over the earth.[7]

The new spirituality retains the old magic of the Sufi mystics, the Sikh *guru*s and Sri Chaitanya, that is, the eternal emotion, love. Love stays back. It opens all doors: the Mother confirms. In a way, Tagore's *Gitanjali* is also spiritual poetry within its mystic form, as he has identified the Divine in the material universe, the Divine whose love would have been meaningless without the human individual.

> Yes, I know, this is nothing but thy love, O beloved of my heart — this golden light that dances upon the leaves, these

7. Ibid., p. 62.

> idle clouds sailing across the sky, this passing breeze leaving its coolness upon my forehead.[8]

Tagore sings the glory of a manifold opportunity in *Gitanjali,* the various feelings in various circumstances, "the moments when the inner lamps are lit and life's cherished guests are left aside,"[9] the moments of death and birth, the moments when chains are broken by the pressure of songs, the moments of yearning for that sweet touch in the allness of the Universe, the moments of discovery of an endless becoming.

> But I find that thy will knows no need in me. And when old words die out on the tongue, new melodies break forth from the heart; and when the old tracks are lost, new country is revealed with its wonders.[10]

Love is the motivating force in this endless walk ahead. Poetry is an accompaniment and music removes the blocks. Love is greater than poetry.

> My poet's vanity dies in shame before thy sight. O master poet, I have sat down at thy feet. Only let me make my life simple and straight, like a flute or reed for thee to fill with music.[11]

One instantly remembers the Mother's *Prayers,* where the theme becomes identical. Leaving the container empty is an invitation to God to fill it up; leaving the page blank is an invitation to God to express Him on that page. The Mother (Mira Alfassa) was using the same theme around 1912 in her famous diary in French entitled *Prières et Méditations.* The English translation

8. Ibid.
9. Sri Aurobindo, *Savitri: A Legend and a Symbol,* Pondicherry, Sri Aurobindo Ashram, Book I, Canto IV, 1950, p. 42.
10. *The English Writings of Rabindranath Tagore,* vol. I, p. 54.
11. Ibid., pp. 44-45.

Prayers and Meditations reads very much like the English *Gitanjali.* Here is a significant prayer-poem from her diary entry dated 20 November 1914:

> Oh, I would be before Thee, Lord, always like an absolutely blank page, so that Thy will may be written in me without any difficulty, any mixture.[12]

Apart from this note, there appears quite often the same gesture of love and surrender in Tagore's English *Gitanjali.* As an aesthete Tagore has his own ways of enjoying every little aspect of life. But who will deny his integral vision in *Gitanjali*? W.B. Yeats sums up Tagore's integral awareness, the sense, which connects Matter and Spirit with an utmost ease and a mellow sensitivity.

> Flowers and rivers, the blowing of conch shells, the heavy rain of the Indian July, or the parching heat, are images of the modes of that heart in union or in separation; and a man sitting in a boat upon a river playing upon a lute, like one of those figures full of mysterious meaning in a Chinese picture, is God Himself.[13]

The new spirituality is all-inclusive; no experience is irrelevant to the quest, only if the voyager is awake to the manifold opportunities to discover the Person behind the Many. Tagore's language moves like a clear cool stream, suggesting a suppressed glory. Only the perceptive reader sees the effort to reach that imprisoned splendour.

---

12. The Mother, Mira Alfassa, *Prayers and Meditations,* Pondicherry, Sri Aurobindo Ashram, 1985, p. 300.
13. *The English Writings of Rabindranath Tagore,* vol. I, p. 40.

10

The Gita and Gitanjali

WAS Tagore aware of the fact that he was practising the Gita's gospel of love as a modern mystic? It is not hard to see that he is, in many ways, presenting his narrator-hero as the God-lover of the *Gita*. Sri Aurobindo's explanation of the aspect of love in the *Gita* confirms the fact that the seeker's "God-vision does not divorce him from life, nor does he miss anything of the fullness of life."[1] Let us listen to Tagore:

> I have had my invitation to this world's festival, and thus my life has been blessed. My eyes have seen and my ears have heard. It was my part at this feast to play upon my instrument and I have done all I could. Now, I ask, has the time come at last when I may go in and see thy face and offer thee my silent salutation?[2]

If this is a very simple way of translating the philosophy of the *Gita* or a way of feeling it in a colourless idiom, then Tagore can also express it in his rich metaphorical style, in his typical Bengali-flavoured English. Let us listen to the last poem in *Gitanjali* (103):

> In one salutation to thee, my God, let all my senses spread out and touch this world at thy feet. Like a rain cloud of July hung low with *its* burden of unshed showers let all my

---

1. Sri Aurobindo, *SABCL*, vol. 13, *Essays on the Gita*, p. 317.
2. *The English Writings of Rabindranath Tagore*, vol. I, New Delhi, Sahitya Akademi, p. 47.

> mind bend down at thy door in one salutation to thee. Let all my songs gather together their diverse strains into a single current and flow to a sea of silence in one salutation to thee. Like a flock of homesick cranes flying night and day back to their mountain nests let all my life take its voyage to its eternal home in one salutation to thee.[3]

This poet too, though not as deeply as Sri Aurobindo, seems to have realized that all life is *yoga*. Tagore does not use the word *yoga*, but the poems in *Gitanjali* speak of his deliberate effort at union with God. This may not be called a very methodized effort towards self-perfection. However, a certain kind of method is throughout there and that may be seen as the *yoga* of devotion, which aims at supernal ecstasy. Sri Aurobindo says, "The principle of Bhakti Yoga is to utilize all the normal relations of human life into which emotion enters and apply them no longer to transient worldly relations, but to the joy of the All-Loving, the All-Beautiful and the All-Blissful. Worship and meditation are used only for the preparation and increase of intensity of the divine relationship."[4] Tagore wishes to increase his intensity of worship through the poems of *Gitanjali*, where worship is art and art is worship. He was surely attempting to write the poetry of absolute self-giving, and even this effort has given his poetry a rare charm. Even if the total self-giving is not there, love of the Highest is a recurring theme in *Gitanjali* and it is precisely this that has infused in it the feeling of Chapter IX of the *Gita*. Sri Aurobindo's commentary on the *Gita* will give us a clear indication of the ultimate goal of Tagore. Towards that final goal the poet of *Gitanjali* was moving in his own brittle ways:

---

3. Ibid., p. 78.
4. Sri Aurobindo, *SABCL*, vol. 20, pp. 33-34.

> To make the mind one with the divine consciousness, to make the whole of our emotional nature one love of God everywhere, to make all our works one sacrifice to the Lord of the worlds and all our worship and aspiration one adoration of him and self-surrender, to direct the whole self Godwards in an entire union is the way to rise out of a mundane into a divine existence. This is the *Gita*'s teaching of divine love and devotion, in which knowledge, works and the heart's longing become one in a supreme unification, a merging of all their divergences, an intertwining of all their threads, a high fusion, a wide identifying movement.[5]

Who can deny this effort in the poet of *Gitanjali*? The exact stage of advance does not matter. His effort is enough proof for us that Tagore was a trendsetter, something like the literary Transcendentalists of America, who had wished to combine vision and beautiful presentation. That relates Tagore to Emerson and Thoreau, who had been steeped in the *Gita*. In poem after poem, Tagore expresses his Godward emotion with a distinct memory of the *Gita*'s gospel of love or devotion or sacrifice or surrender:

> I shall ever try to drive all evils away from my heart and keep my love in flower, knowing that thou hast thy seat in the inmost shrine of my heart. And it shall be my endeavour to reveal thee in my actions, knowing it is thy power gives me strength to act.[6]

Love, action and knowledge are synthesized in a supreme gesture of sacrifice, which is just a synonym for love in Sri Aurobindo's *yoga*. It is also a kind of replacement: the expulsion of evil and the installation of love. Throughout *Gitanjali*, there is a deliberate effort at what the Mother would

5. Sri Aurobindo, *SABCL*, vol. 13, pp. 321-22.
6. *The English Writings of Rabindranath Tagore*, vol. I, p. 44.

have called a "reversal of consciousness."[7] Even the effort gave birth to a rare art, which shook the literary world in 1913. From Tagore's subliminal came all those finer aspirations and strivings towards a better self. And it was also an indefinable pressure of love, at least a partial opening of the psychic being. *Gitanjali* seems to have been influenced by the doctrine of sacrifice quite common in the Indian scriptures, which the *Gita* seeks to put in a capsule form. Ego creates all the intricacies. Hence, we see the quest for simplicity and straightforwardness in poem no. 7. Tagore knows well the distinctions between desire and love. He knows the result of desire. He knows the value of surrender, the art of feeling the best kind of relief. That is why some of the poems may be read as prefatory notes to the Mother's *Prayers and Meditations.* Desires block his movement. But, he has the consciousness to feel that God is merciful in his hard refusals. He is not frustrated by his desire and incapacity, because he loves and is confident of an answering love. Hope, faith and joy mingle with his love. To love truly is to know and work in the true spirit. Once again Sri Aurobindo's explanation of the supreme word of the *Gita* will throw light on Tagore's way of love:

> The whole consciousness becomes full of the Godhead and replete with his answering consciousness; the whole life flows into one sea of bliss-experience. All the speech and thought of such God-lovers becomes a mutual utterance and understanding of the Divine. In that one joy is concentrated all the contentment of the being, all the play and pleasure of the nature. There is a continual union from moment to moment in the thought and memory, there is an unbroken continuity of the experience of oneness in the spirit.[8]

7. *Questions and Answers,* 1950-51, CWM, vol. 4, p. 19.
8. Sri Aurobindo, *SABCL,* vol. 13, p. 339.

Sri Aurobindo has been speaking on love up till now. Then there is a subtle turn in his argument. He brings in the other two aspects of *yoga* — work and knowledge — which must be synthesized with devotion. Let us listen to that before relating the point of synthesis to Tagore's poems:

> And from the moment that this inner state begins, even in the stage of imperfection, the Divine confirms it by the perfect *yoga* of the will and intelligence. He uplifts the blazing lamp of knowledge within us, he destroys the ignorance of the separative mind and will, he stands revealed in the human spirit. By the *yoga* of the will and intelligence founded on an illumined union of works and knowledge the transition was effected from our lower troubled mind-ranges to the immutable calm of the witnessing Soul above the active nature. But now by this greater *yoga* of the *buddhi* founded on an illumined union of love and adoration with an all-comprehending knowledge the soul rises in a vast ecstasy to the whole transcendental truth of the absolute and all-originating Godhead. The Eternal is fulfilled in the individual spirit and individual nature; the individual spirit is exalted from birth in time to the infinitudes of the Eternal.[9]

The *yoga* of love is being supported by knowledge (intelligence) and action. Sri Aurobindo differentiates between love and adoration; he wants to see them fused in this way to form the integral union between man and God. As an authentic interpreter of the *Gita*, Sri Aurobindo virtually clarifies the journey of another spiritual seeker aspiring to reach the goal of the human journey. In poem no. 25, Tagore echoes the Mother's prayer of 5 December 1912, where she says that even the effort becomes an obstacle in a wrong gesture of action and intelligence creating a link-failure in love:

---

9. Ibid., pp. 339-40.

> Yes, we should not put too much intensity, too much effort into our seeking for Thee; the effort and intensity become a veil in front of Thee; we must not desire to see Thee, for that is still a mental agitation which obscures Thy Eternal Presence. . . .[10]

In a sudden moment of the soul, Tagore catches something of that truth in poem no. 25. In an ideal synthesis of true love, true action and true knowledge, Tagore realizes the value of trust, surrender and waiting without impatience of any kind. An Aurobindonian will be thrilled to listen to the words of Tagore:

> Let me not force my flagging spirit into a poor preparation for thy worship.[11]

The poet of *Gitanjali* was living in the spirit of the *Gita*.

Forceful discipline is a fearful thing for Tagore. It does not go with his temperament. Again and again, in his prose, poetry and plays, he speaks against the repression of natural impulses. The *Gita,* too, disapproves of an ascetic discipline and favours the state of equilibrium. A careful observation will show that Tagore, unlike the Vaisnavites, has maintained a kind of quiet and peace and equilibrium in his love for the Divine. Nothing purifies more than the instant installation of the Divine in one's heart. Tagore seems to have known this simple truth. But then, he seems to have known a key principle suggested in the *Gita,* the principle of balance at the time of offering to the Divine as a great gesture of sacrifice.

Interpreters of the *Gita,* who had worked on the text prior to Sri Aurodindo, had not illumined properly the issue of sacrifice or love and quietude lying concealed in the great

---

10. *Prayers and Meditations,* CWM, vol. I, p. 10.

11. *The English Writings of Rabindranath Tagore,* vol. I, p. 50.

Sanskrit text. The true attitude came to Tagore naturally or maybe he too understood the value of peaceful devotion latent in the *Gita*. The surrender must be quiet and peaceful and then only one loses all wrong vibrations for any other creature. One is approaching a vast quietude and therefore peace and quiet must be the essential gestures from the human individual. Sri Aurobindo describes the aspect of surrender or sacrifice in the light of the *Gita*.

> The supreme faith is that which sees God in all and to its eye the manifestation and the non-manifestation are one Godhead. The perfect union is that which meets the Divine at every moment, in every action and with all the integrality of the nature.[12]

It is "the calm soul of knowledge that sees the one self in all things,"[13] Sri Aurobindo clarifies a little later and then uses a very relevant phrase, "the tranquil ego-less equality."[14] Tagore was virtually seeking to live out this phrase without knowing the theoretical subtleties of the *yoga* of duration. He practised the natural *yoga* of duration in *Gitanjali*.

> Let only that little be left of my will whereby I may feel thee on every side, and come to thee in everything, and offer to thee my love every moment.[15]

This is the constant remembrance or the constant sacrifice of which the *Gita* speaks frequently, and we should not also miss to see that Tagore has followed here the conditions of peace and quiet as latent in the deeper texture of the *Gita*. In the *Gitanjali* prayer, which we have quoted above, one finds that

---

12. Sri Aurobindo, *SABCL*, vol. 13, p. 386.
13. Ibid., p. 391.
14. Ibid.
15. *The English Writings of Rabindranath Tagore*, vol. I, p. 53.

quiet gesture of aspiration leading to an integral surrender ("may feel thee on every side," and "come to thee in everything"). Knowingly or unknowingly or half consciously Tagore was following the *Gita*'s doctrine of integral surrender in the *Gitanjali*. There is no hurried gesture in the book. The aspiration runs through the poems in a gesture of waiting. Tagore feels all life as his life. He feels that his limbs are made glorious by the touch of the world of life and that silence is gold.

> No more noisy, loud words from me — such is my Master's will.[16]

The poet of *Gitanjali* aspires for death on the way to his beloved.

16. Ibid., p. 73.

11

Tagore and the Prophecy in Savitri
Book X, Canto 4

SAVITRI is quite far from the sweet mysticism that we see in the poetry of Tagore, whose heroines do not wish to rise beyond the mundane self and refuse to grow in the higher nature. Chitra's confession indicates that the woman in Tagore chooses to remain a woman instead of aspiring for the Supernature:

> I am Chitra. No goddess to be worshipped. . . . If you deign to keep me by your side in the path of danger and daring, if you allow me to share the great duties of your life, then you will know my true self.[1]

The truth of this "true self" is Tagore's own perception of life. Sri Aurobindo's Savitri searches for a wider self and grows into a vaster spiritual figure. The concept of the World Mother has not been a usual vision for Tagore. Yet, there are times in Tagore's plays, when the woman reacts to the world with a sharp feeling of pain, as in *Malini*. But then, Malini suffers from a weak psychic being inside her. One sees her incapacity as compared to the positive approach of Sri Aurobindo's heroine, who is bent on changing the complexion of the earth. Here is the helpless stance of Tagore's Malini:

> Now that I have met the world face to face my heart has grown timid, and I do not know how to hold the helm of the

---

1. *The English Writings of Rabindranath Tagore*, vol. II, pp. 50-51.

> great ship that I must guide. I feel I am alone, and the world is large, and ways are many, and the light from the sky comes of a sudden to vanish the next moment.[2]

Sri Aurobindo's Savitri is an embodiment of strength. She is *shakti,* who saves. She is Light, who illumines. She is creatrix, who leads to the supramental victory. In Sri Aurobindo's epic, she is a round character evolving throughout the poem and comes out of her veil in Book X: poetry and drama come together in a moment of cosmic conflict.

The final debate of love and death sheds significant light on Sri Aurobindo's concern for material life and his vision of the future of earth, which is now a polluted and plundered planet continuously living under the shadow of death and doom. It is the most dramatic part of the epic, as the Lord of Death (Yama) puts up his final resistance against the daughter of Light, who is also Love. The speeches are long, but unlike Shelley or Tagore, Sri Aurobindo knows how to create that sense of tension, which is essential for dramatic poetry. Between the arguments and counter-arguments of Death and Savitri, there is a masterful narrator, who intensifies the cosmic tension between the two powerful forces. Death had always had the final word. Only, this time it was going to end on a different note.

Love walks behind death with her claim and reaches a new landscape of despair. It is a flashback to the futile history of the earth. The narrator's voice runs to 86 lines culminating in the phrase "fruitless labours of the worlds," which leads us to Death's viewpoint. Mind is man; beyond thought he cannot soar. He sees the greater heavens; he cannot mount to those

---

2. Ibid., p. 80, For all other quotations see *Savitri*: *A Legend and a Symbol, SABCL,* vol. 29, The lines quoted stand between pp. 648-67.

peaks. Failing in his attempts, he seeks *nirvana*. The earth remains as it is, unchanged. How can one plant on earth the living Truth or make the world of Matter the home of God? Truth never appears; only the thought of Truth is our reality. We know only the name of God, not him. If there is a God, he does not care for the world. He is cool, indifferent; he enjoys the distress of man. He is solitary; he does not care for man's love. His laws are fixed. How shall the mighty Mother change his laws? Death tempts Savitri with the dreams of personal salvation, God's "immobile peace."

Savitri is quick to see the falsity of this argument, the false light called into blind Truth's eyes. With the World-Mother housed within her, she cannot turn to eternal peace leaving the unchanged earth behind. And she refuses to believe that the world is cut-off from Truth and God. She refers to her mind as a torch lit from the eternal sun, her life as a breath drawn from the immortal Guest and her body as the Eternal's house. Then through her mouth Sri Aurobindo, the bio-scientist and the anthropologist, sums up his theory of evolution, which suggests that man is not an end-product in Nature's lab; he is a transitional creature:

> If in the meaningless Void creation rose,
> If from a bodiless Force Matter was born,
> If Life could climb in the unconscious tree,
> If green delight break into emerald leaves
> And its laughter of beauty blossom in the flower,
> If sense could wake in tissue, nerve and cell,
> And Thought seize the grey matter of the brain,
> And soul peep from its secrecy through the flesh,
> How shall the nameless light not leap on men,
> And unknown powers emerge from Nature's sleep?

Man is entrusted with a great task, the task of creating that new species, which is bound to come because Nature cannot remain satisfied with the creation of an imperfect being. That is why Savitri is so assertive in her speech. She strongly believes that the transition from man to another new species is no utopia, as the signs of the super-race are already visible on earth. Savitri stands erect before the Lord of Death and points towards herself as a living example of Supernature:

> I am not bound by thought or sense or shape;
> I live in the glory of the Infinite,
> I am near to the Nameless and Unknowable,
> The Ineffable is now my household mate.
> But standing on Eternity's luminous brink
> I have discovered that the world was He;
> I have met Spirit with spirit, Self with self,
> But I have loved too the body of my God.
> I have pursued him in his earthly form.
> A lonely freedom cannot satisfy
> A heart that has grown one with every heart:
> I am a deputy of the aspiring world,
> My spirit's liberty I ask for all.

Death's rhetoric seeks to frustrate her. It presents a false image of Savitri's power, the image of a powerful but restless force. There is a note of threatening in Yama's directive:

> Touch not the seated lines, the ancient laws,
> Respect the calm of great established things.

Savitri re-interprets the idea of calm ironically for the Lord of Death. True calm is not inertia or the suppression of the vital or a halt. The soul is on the move; it naturally yearns for the new and the unknown. Savitri responds to the directive of Death with a Blakean command:

> Impose not upon sentient minds and hearts
> The dull fixity that binds inanimate things. . . .
> Man turns to a nobler walk, a master path.

Sri Aurobindo alludes to Shelley's Prometheus in the next line with the words "I trample on thy law with living feet" and then passes on to a more powerful dramatic debate. Savitri says, "I claim from Time my will's eternity, God from his moments." Death promptly puts a rhetorical question, the question of the past ascetics who had enjoyed withdrawal:

> Why should the noble and immortal will
> Stoop to the petty works of transient earth,
> Freedom forgotten and the Eternal's path?

Death mocks Savitri for having rejected the gods in favour of man. Savitri's next speech claims that God approves of her love for earth. Why are we here then? Why did he give his passion to me?

> If not to achieve, to flower in me, to love,
> Carving his human image richly shaped
> In thoughts and largeness and golden powers?

Earth was a difficult production, not heaven. Amidst the ominous masks and the terrible forces of earth, it is real greatness to create gods. Death's next speech accepts the presence of the World-Mother in Savitri, but he still goes on denying her claim. This is the most poetic speech from the Lord of Death and it images the despair of material life very convincingly. How can Truth invade the sense-life? How is it possible to integrate Matter and Spirit?

> Two Powers real but to each other untrue,
> Two consort stars in the mooned night of mind
> That towards two opposite horizons gaze,
> The white head and black tail of the mystic drake,
> The swift and the lame foot, wing strong, wing broken. . . .

Death negatives the idea that Eternal Truth may live with mortal men. He puts up a challenge before Savitri:

Or if she dwells within thy mortal heart,
Show me the body of the living Truth
Or draw for me the outline of her face
That I too may obey and worship her.
Then will I give thee back thy Satyavan. . . .
No magic Truth can bring the dead to life,
No power of earth cancel the thing once done,
No joy of the heart can last surviving death,
No bliss persuade the past to live again.

Savitri, of course, is not affected by the anaphoral "No." She wakes up into a greater light to see that Death is God and yet not he; Death is "only his own black shadow on his path." Further clarifications glorify her speech:

Two contraries needed for his great World-task,
Two poles whose currents wake the immense World-Force.

The speech lingers to show how all contraries prepare for harmony and then to map the ladder of transcendence — (1) The Higher Mind, (2) The Illumined Mind, (3) The Intuition, and (4) The Overmind (which is a gateway to the Supermind) — and finally to indicate the role of the World-Mother in the transformation of the earth-consciousness.

The Lord of Death raises his voice for the last time to challenge the "human claimant to immortality":

Reveal thy power, lay bare thy spirit's force,
Then will I give back to thee Satyavan.

It is time for Savitri to show him who she is. Sri Aurobindo uses cinematic technique to project the change in the human figure:

In a flaming moment of apocalypse
The Incarnation thrust aside its veil.

A little figure in infinity
Yet stood and seemed the Eternal's very house,
As if the world's centre was her very soul
And all wide space was but its outer robe.

The narrative goes on to highlight the power and the glory of the woman, who wakes up the sleeping serpent within. When the exposition ends, the narrator completes his adoration with a wonderful apophthegm:

Eternity looked into the eyes of Death,
And Darkness saw God's living Reality.

Savitri ends the cosmic dialogue, as the Great Mother speaks through her explaining that she has appointed Death to force the soul of man to struggle for Light. The Incarnation keeps him in the job for man's assistance, but bids him release the soul of Satyavan, who is man's representative in the house of God. The captain wishes man to follow his track to immortality.

The last battle starts; the two oppose each other, face to face. Sri Aurobindo helps us see the cosmic combat:

His being like a huge fort of darkness towered;
Around it her light grew, an ocean's siege.

There are other fantastic visuals like the light's "burning tongue" licking up Death and the light finally eating the body of Yama, who has frantically and vainly called for help from the Night, Hell and the Inconscient. Curiously enough the body of Death is not burnt to ashes, but enlightened by the fire of love.

Canto IV in Book X is an experiment in modern poetic drama dealing with an ancient myth. The form is a queer blend of the objective and the authorial voice. The interesting thing about the canto is the fact that a cosmic dramatist standing at the summit of spirituality looks back to the earth with an absolute commitment. Beyond the landscape of post-modernism, there wakes up a memory of the future, a prescient dream of a smiling earth.

12

Tagore's Paintings
A Consciousness Approach

WHILE Sri Aurobindo was fascinated by the art and architecture of ancient and medieval India, Tagore turned to the modern West as a painter and wished his friends and relations to go to Japan and to the Western countries to elevate the status of their paints. Sri Aurobindo searched for the spiritual touch in Indian paints. Tagore, the painter, indulged in the vital consciousness in his weird paintings and drawings. He is, arguably, the first modern painter of India. He is a pilgrim of Night without the vision of Paradiso. He never encouraged national boasting in the field of art, although he did not resist this revivalistic trend in the wake of the renaissance. Not that he relied much on colonial art. But, he was not in favour of all Indianness in art:

> When we speak of Indian art it indicates some truth based upon the Indian tradition and temperament. At the same time we must know that there is no such thing as absolute caste restriction in human cultures; they have the power to combine and produce new variations, and such combinations have been going on for ages, proving the truth of the deep unity of human psychology.[1]

A preference for a purely nationalistic painting was there in the early part of his career. He loved Ravi Varma's paints

1. *Visva-Bharati Quarterly*, May, 1935.

because of their Indianness. In the 1890s Indian subjects and sculptures with Indian mood and flavour meant much to him. Later, after the partition of Bengal, the nationalistic stress passed away giving way to modernism, which came to him first naturally and then from Japan and the Western countries. In a letter to Gaganendranath Tagore, dated 8 August 1916, Tagore is indirectly critical about the limitations of Indian art. "When are you going to come out of home to embrace the greater world?"[2] In the same letter, and also in a letter to Rathindranath Tagore written on 22 August of the same year, there is a reference to a Japanese artist named *Araai* whom Tagore was planning to send to Calcutta as a trainer.[3] Tagore thought Gaganendranath and others needed to learn the finer points of Japanese art very urgently. He was fascinated by the blend of art and utilitarian values in Japanese art. Every small thing was beautiful. The Indians could not do that. The Japanese people made life beautiful in its totality. Where did the Japanese hide their rubbish? he wondered. It was sheer joy for him to see how the Japanese women did everything neatly and with an authentic touch of Beauty.[4] In the letter to Rathindranath Tagore, the criticism was direct and constructive:

> In the art of modern Bengal, I persistently feel the need of a little more of force, courage and wideness. We have given stress on minor things — very insignificant things . . . Gagan and Aban are reluctant to come here. Is there no possibility

---

2. Letter to Gaganendranath Tagore, 8 August 1916, (tr. by the author).
3. Letter to Rathindranath Tagore, 22 August 1916, (tr. by the author).
4. Letter to Gaganendranath Tagore, 8 August 1916, (tr. by the author).

> of Nandalal's visit here? Coming here I have felt that the Japanese have no parallel in the field of painting.[5]

Tagore was all praise for Japanese painting on large canvas and wished Nandalal Bose and others to learn that art from Japanese painters. While Sri Aurobindo was seeking to encourage the nation to revive the ancient and medieval art tradition of India, Tagore was distinctly seeking to initiate the Indian painters to the principles of modernism. As a practising painter and art-critic Tagore was not interested in spirituality; he was interested in the trendy modernism, which was strongly vitalistic in nature. In poetry and other arts, Sri Aurobindo's aim was one-pointed: the Spirit must be expressed through all kinds of art.

He too appreciated the Japanese, but because he found in Japanese art the inner principles, the noiseless art consecrated to the Divine.

> A great oriental work of art does not easily reveal its secret to one who comes to it solely in a mood of aesthetic curiosity or with a considering critical objective mind, still less as the cultivated and interested tourist passing among strange and foreign things; but it has to be seen in loneliness, in the solitude of one's self, in moments when one is capable of long and deep meditation and as little weighted as possible with the conventions of material life. That is why the Japanese with their fine sense in these things, — a sense which modern Europe with her assault of crowded art galleries and over-pictured walls seems to have quite lost, though perhaps I am wrong, and those are the right conditions for display of European art — have put their temples and their Buddhas as often as possible away on mountains and in distant or secluded scenes of Nature and

5. Letter to Rathindranath Tagore, 22 August 1916, (tr. by the author).

> avoid living with great paintings in the crude hours of daily life. . . .[6]

This and many other passages from *The Foundations of Indian Culture* speak of a new aesthetic principle born of the old credo of the ancient Indians: Art must express the Divine. "Its highest business is to disclose something of the Self, the Infinite, the Divine to the regard of the soul, the Self through its expressions, the Infinite through its living finite symbols, the Divine through his powers."[7]

Tagore, certainly not a spiritualist in the field of painting, believed that the contemporary Indian paintings had nothing to do with society. In 1928, at age 67, Tagore began to draw and paint with a queer enthusiasm. He had done some occasional doodles and sketches in the past, but now it was a serious affair and he was athirst for fame as a painter. The craving for fame was as vital as his weird paintings. The late partiality for an unknown art forced poetry out of his life. Tagore explained to Nirmal Kumari that the main reason of its attraction lay in a kind of mysterious unexpectedness. In poetry, he believed, rhythm came beforehand, at least faintly, and after that rhythm flew out smoothly "as the Ganga had flown out from the locks of Shiva." In painting it is just the opposite — the line appeared as he kept the pen on the paper and then the more a shape appeared the more it moved towards the head. His mind wondered at this strange creation:

> . . . If I were a competent artist, I would have preconceived my paints. In that case, the interior scheme would have taken an external shape. There is a joy in that too. But then it is more intoxicating when the mind is absorbed in external

6. *SABCL,* vol. 14, pp. 212-13.
7. Ibid., p. 208.

> creation. The result is a total withdrawal from all external activities. If like those days spent by the Padma I were totally free from duty so as to produce only paintings for the Golden Boat of Time! Now I can give little time to that because of the pressure of various duties. That little is not enough to satisfy my mind. It wishes to occupy the whole of my leisure. I am also keen on giving my consent. The stars obstruct. One of them is the welfare of mankind.[8]

This is obviously a problem of integrating aesthetics with life, which is not at all a problem with Sri Aurobindo at any stage of his life. He worked coolly and did not care for appraisals or publicity. He just enjoyed the joy of creation. Tagore was fond of indicating at times that painting linked him up with God and that it was God who was creating his new boundaries in limitless mysterious lines. The joy of paint is the joy of the finite, he wrote to Nirmal Kumari. In the discipline of his paint, he saw the Presence clearly.[9] How true was Tagore in this claim for vital inspiration? In any case, he wished to equate his joy of painting with divine inspiration. In the letter written to Sudhindranath Dutta on 1 April 1930 there is a very distinct desire for fame. This is very vital and does not go with the Mother's and Sri Aurobindo's ideal of an artist.

> I cannot stand the remarks of the underqualified. Hope your letter to Rothenstein won't be futile. I too will talk to him on that when I meet him. I am not sure whether he can do it or not. When I *go* to Oxford I will renew my contacts. I'll also try my luck in the Continent. Today I'll raise the issue before my German friend.[10]

---

8. Letter to Nirmal Kumari Mohalanabish, 8 November 1928, (tr. by the author).
9. Letter to Nirmal Kumari, 30 November 1928, (tr. by the author).
10. Letter to Sudhindranath Dutta, 1 April 1930, (tr. by the author).

This is not the only example. In letter after letter, he expressed his restlessness and passion for fame in that new field. On 17 May 1930, he wrote to Sudhindranath Dutta:

> My fame as a painter in Paris might have reached the ears of my countrymen. I wish you were here. My paints are going to be exhibited in London and Birmingham. The connoisseurs who have seen them, have been appreciative. This time I hope to be greeted with either a garland or a certificate when I return home.[11]

He wanted more time for his paints and lamented that it was not there because of his public engagements. In the 1930s, he virtually became child-like in his interest in the new game. And sometimes, there came out the typical efflux of a dissatisfied romantic.

> . . . My eyes have strained enough and now they must last for my paints. I found my paints at the twilight of my life. In the approaching night of my life, I thought of a honeymoon with painting. I wished to sport with her in absolute quiet .My paints are being affected by my workload and people around me. Meanwhile, my eyesight is failing.[12]

There are about two thousand and five hundred available paintings by Tagore, mostly done between 1928 and 1940. There are also quite a few self-portraits; there are faces, landscapes and nudes and other varieties, most of which are the products of the creative vital. Prithwish Neogy beautifully sums up the topics, which point to what Sri Aurobindo calls the "subliminal":[13]

11. Letter to Sudhindranath Dutta, 17 May 1930.
12. Letter to Amiya Chakraborty, 1938, date and month unknown. All these letters are translated by the author for this book.
13. "Subliminal" is a general term used by Sri Aurobindo for all parts of the being which are not on the waking surface. See *SABCL*, vol. 22, p. 354 for Sri Aurobindo's explanation.

> Unfurling, animated ribbons, composite flower-birds, nameless archaistic beastliness, ambiguous sardonic imps, contorting primitive reptiles, proliferating monster-vessels, oddly sensuous nudes on extravagant furniture, improbable protagonists in a mysterious melodrama, distraught angular pilgrims on an unknown quest eternal, romantic dream houses, illustrations to lost stories, lovers, silhouettes, incandescent evening landscapes, murderous enactments, peaceful promenades, familiar types, characters and portraits, masks of sarcasm, masks of terror, heads of power and glory, delicate, oval moon-faces of silent lips and with eyes to transfix. All freshly formed, rampant, iridescent.[14]

Unlike the recurring theme of mystical quest in his poetry, songs and in some plays like *The Post Office* and *Malini,* the paintings usually come from the zone located between the heart and the sex-centre, the most problematic zone in the human consciousness. The paintings are as secular as his later poems. Buddhadeva Bose observes: "The usual order is reversed in him: the older he grew, the more secular he becomes."[15] Sisirkumar Ghose thinks in another way as he talks of Tagore's later poetry, which is quite often seen together with the weird paints. Let us see how Ghose sums up the essence of the later poetry:

> Here is a grappling with the powers of Darkness not merely in the manner of a metaphor but in dead earnest, something especially and excruciatingly real, something that endows them with the majesty of archetypal poetry, ample recompense for the lesser things in the midst of which they

---

14. Prithwish Neogi, "Drawings and Paintings of Rabindranath Tagore" in *Rabindranath Tagore: A Centenary Volume 1861-1961,* Sahitya Akademi, p. 201.

15. Buddhadeva Bose, *An Acre of Green Grass,* p. 12.

> shine in such sombre splendour. In them "a terrible beauty is born." These are, as Whitman might say, poems retrieved from the night.[16]

The words may be applied to Tagore's paints quite relevantly. It is natural to remember the poetry of Baudelaire as we look at the gloomy paints of Tagore. Both the artists know how to extract beauty from filth and mire.

---

16. Sisirkumar Ghose, *The Later Poems of Tagore*, Sterling, New Delhi, 1989, p. 193.

13

The Viziers of Bassora
Sri Aurobindo's Shakespeariana

WHILE the resistance against Sri Aurobindo's poetry has weakened during the last ten years, funny remarks about his dramatic experiments continue to appear in the critical studies on Indo-Anglian literature. Citations would take a lot of space. Hence my gist: "Sri Aurobindo's plays are imitative and they are not meant for the stage." Guide-books meant for the Post-Graduate classes carry that "wise" judgement to our students. Their makers do not care — in most cases — to know what Prof. Iyengar and Dr Prema Nandakumar have to say on those plays. I would like to draw the attention of the reader to one of the early plays, entitled *The Viziers of Bassora*: *A Dramatic Romance,* just to indicate what kind of artistic seriousness had worked behind that happy comedy. Unlike Tagore, Sri Aurobindo follows the classical and Shakespearean principles of drama.

In *The Viziers of Bassora,* he seems to remember Aristophanes, Terence, Kalidasa and Shakespeare from time to time, even though he is enjoying a walk through the middle-east corridors, the filthy and fragrant zones of Bassora and Baghdad. The source lies in *Arabian Nights Entertainments,* which Sri Aurobindo won as a school prize in England. K.R.S. Iyengar observes:

> *The Viziers* is principally based on "The Tale of the Beautiful Sweet-Friend," a delightful yarn that Shahrazad spins out over nearly six nights. Sri Aurobindo, however, introduced a few changes in the story and added some new characters as well, partly to purify the story of some of its prurience and partly to underline the principle of contrast in the characterization.[1]

But then, some of the lower vital stuff remain in Sri Aurobindo's play reminding us of the European comic playwrights and a coarse comic imagination, which was prevalent in the nineteenth-century Bengali literature of the pre-Bankim era.

The story may be summed up as a play of Morality, but that will hide three original elements: the poetry, the humour and the invented speech for every individual which marks the consciousness of a character. Two viziers of Bassora, Alfazzal (good) and Almuene (bad), and their sons Nureddene (good but unrestrained) and Fareed (deformed and vulgar and cruel like his father) fight over a slave girl (Anice), who is a paragon of beauty. Alfazzal buys her for the king and his son Nureddene falls for her. Anice reciprocates and the lenient father unites them and leaves Bassora for a time, dividing his property between his son and his wife, afraid that Nureddene will squander away his money. Which he does. Nureddene is trapped by Almuene and when he is about to lose Anice, he decides to leave for Baghdad. Haroun-al-Rasheed, Caliph of Baghdad, sends Nureddene back to Bassora with a letter to the king (his cousin) to help him and shelters Anice in his palace. Nureddene is taken captive and just when he is going to be executed, Haroun appears to rescue him. Nureddene

---

1. K.R. Srinivasa Iyengar, *Sri Aurobindo — A Biography and a History*, 1972, pp. 121-22.

replaces the bad king. The Caliph, the Providence of "Allah's Vicegerent" speaks the last sweet words of wisdom.

Like Shakespeare, young Aurobindo is an elusive playwright. The budding *rishi* veils himself behind the vital creatures of Bassora and Baghdad. The play was written between his late 1920s and early 1930s. One suspects he was creating Shakespeariana for a post-modern audience. I use the word post-modern intentionally, because some of the speeches used in the play anticipate the perverted idiom of the twenty-first century, when we have lost all our ability to hide the animal in us. Did Aurobindo Ghose really hear people speak like that in the late 1890s and in the early years of the twentieth century or did he know about the real speech-style used in those fantastic cities?

All perversions of speech flare up with a new colour under the masterful touch of the playwright's comic imagination. While Tagore is a master of symbolic drama, he is un-Shakespearean in his inability to discover proper speech-styles for most of his characters. Poetry and action seldom come together in the great Bengali poet, who does not know how to write multi-dimensional poetry. Young Aurobindo could do that masterfully in *The Viziers of Bassora* by imaging the characters properly with the help of different speech-styles. Every character is individualized.

Each character projects his/her consciousness through the speeches. Hatred, lust, jealousy, sadism, hypocrisy, frivolity, mixed with perversion of the vital and the mental, flattery and boldness, kindness, the female revolting against the male and the female appreciating the refined virtues in the male, kingship and ethics, the common chords of life leading to a better state of enlightenment — all are there in a social drama of engaging conflict. And there is love: a blend of the

Kalidasian, the Shakespearean and the Aurobindonian tastes.

Young Aurobindo remembers the Shakespearean ambience and recreates it without copying the Bard of Avon. Doonya, Nureddene's cousin, forms a romantic pair with Anice, like Celia and Rosalind. Her words to Anice in Act II, Scene I, have a distinct Shakespearean ring in a new setting:

> You living sweet romance, you come from Persia.
> 'Tis there, I think, they fall in love at sight?[2]

The Duke of *Measure for Measure* comes back as Haroun, the disguised Caliph of Bagdad. This masked Providence comes much later in Sri Aurobindo's play, in Act IV, Scene iii and therefore he does not give us the impression of Shakespeare's string-pulling supremos, the Duke and Prospero. In *The Viziers of Bassora,* there are many unassorted attitudes, a thing usual in Shakespeare's best plays. The voice of the playwright in the last speech of Haroun is in harmony with the Caliph's earlier speech-style. It is natural in the context and does not break the spell of negative capability.

Anice-Aljalice, the slave-girl-turned-heroine, has something of the mellow frankness and wit of Rosalind, but in her despair she does not speak like Rosalind or Isabella. She is Aurobindo Ghose's own creation. Isabella's bitter gesture "Oh, I will go to him and pluck out his eyes!"[3] is not the stance of young Aurobindo's Anice-Aljalice. Here is the voice of a powerful woman in Act V, scene v:

> Caliph, high sovereign, Haroun al Rasheed,
> Men call thee Just, Great Abbasside! I am
> A poor and helpless slave-girl, but my grief
> Is greater than a King. Lord, I demand

---

2. Sri Aurobindo, *SABCL*, vol. 7, Collected Plays, p. 592.
3. *Measure for Measure,* Act IV, Sc. iii, l. 116.

My soul's dear husband at thy hand, who sent him
Alone, unfollowed, without guard or friend
To a tyrant Sultan and more tyrant Vizier,
His potent enemies. Oh, they have killed him!
Give back my husband to my arms unhurt
Or I will rise upon the judgement day
Against thee, Caliph Haroun al Rasheed,
Demanding him at that eternal throne
Where names are not received, nor earthly pomps
Considered. Then my frail and woman's voice
Shall ring more dreadful in thy mighty hearing
Than doom's own trumpet. Answer my demand.[4]

This is the real Aurobindonian woman, whom we see fully developed in *Savitri.* Anice knows at the back of her mind that this Caliph is pious; she knows his foolishness in sending her husband back to Bassora with just a letter to the king; she knows the need for an immediate action from the Caliph; she knows her speech is action. A superior intelligence is at work behind this sincere rhetoric. Although afraid, she wishes to act positively by threatening the Caliph with the power of a woman's love. Later, before the close of the play, when the tension is released, the Caliph reminds Anice of her threatening words. Once again in Act V, Scene vii, there is a hint at a powerful feminine force:

I never was so scared in all my life
As when you rose against me.[5]

This mingling of the opposites — like realism and romance, the tragic and the comic, crudity and refinement, the vulgar and the sublime — is the basis of Shakespeariana. A Lord in *All's Well That Ends Well* sums up the integral view simply:

---

4. Sri Aurobindo, *SABCL,* vol. 7, p. 722.

5. Ibid., p. 735.

> The web of our life is of a mingled yarn,
> Good and ill together.[6]

Sri Aurobindo seems to have known this early in his literary career. Negative capability does not mean that the reader will never know the author's voice in any part of the play. It means the game of the dramatic artist, who invites, as if playfully, the reader or the spectator to find him out in the midst of various unassorted attitudes. The audience is allowed to feel from the start that Bassora was once a seat of culture and that there was a lot of good in the early Moslem polity. People violated culture and yet there were people who knew honestly that "in Islam all men are equal underneath the King."[7] Women were not free and yet there were among the populace, those who held in high esteem the pattern of an educated woman, the image of a Muslim Rosalind. In Act I, Scene iii, Muazzim, the slave trader, introduces the slave girl to Alfazzal, who has not seen her yet:

> You shall not see her equal in a century.
> She has the Koran and the law by heart;
> Song, motion, music and calligraphy
> Are natural to her, and she contains
> All science in one corner of her mind;
> Yet learning less than wit; and either lost
> In the mere sweetness of her speech and beauty.
> You'll hardly have her within fifteen thousand;
> She is a nonpareil.[8]

The same woman has appeared in another shape before another gaze. That shows how masterfully the characters are differentiated through their speeches. Fareed, Almuene's son,

---

6. *All's Well That Ends Well*, Act IV, Sc. iii, l. 67.
7. Sri Aurobindo, *SABCL*, vol. 7, p. 567.
8. Ibid., p. 578.

who wishes his father to buy Anice for him, sees her according to his own nature:

> Such hands! such eyes! such hips! such legs! I am
> Impatient till my elbows meet around her.[9]

Alfazzal sees her as a disguised Peri, who has descended from heaven. Nureddene's initial response is very vital, but his speeches change gradually, with his attachment becoming finer in the later scenes. His cousin, Doonya, speaks of her romantically almost in the idiom of Tagore. The English language and the Bengali sensibility have been happily fused in the following speech in Act I, Scene iv:

> There is a sea of laughter in your body;
> I find it billowing there beneath the calm
> And rippling sweetly out in smiles. . .[10]

Aurobindo Ghose was also under the spell of that leisurely romantic imagination in his twenties and early thirties. Although not quite frequent in Tagore in his early youth, in his mid-life poetry and plays this refined loquacity appears again and again. We find the voice in *Red Oleanders* distinctly affected by this romantic fever:

> On your face, there is the play of life in your eyes and lips; at the back of you flows your black hair, the silent fall of death. The other day when my hands sank into it they felt the soft calm of dying. I long to sleep with my face hidden inside those thick black clusters. You don't know how tired I am![11]

This is a characteristic efflux of Tagore, which is in harmony with the symbolic texture of his plays. Sri Aurobindo, who is using the Shakespearean model in a new age, uses it

9. Ibid., p. 571.
10. Ibid., p. 590.
11. Sisir Kumar Das, ed., *The English Writings*, vol. II, p. 232.

occasionally to indicate the consciousness of certain characters. When he puts this rhetoric in Doonya's mouth, he is certainly thinking of a jovial and good-natured girl with plenty of emotion hidden beneath. Dr Prema Nandakumar draws our attention to the cluster of "likeable" and "good women" in the play: Doonya, Anice, Ameena, Khatoon and the slaves Balkis and Mymoona.[12] Sri Aurobindo, at that stage of his life, might have been fond of the legend of good women in a male dominated world. However, the artist in him made them all individual women with the help of the speeches reflecting their different life-motives. Sri Aurobindo believed that this unbalanced world would have gone to blazes much earlier and that it was only humour, which saved it from catastrophe. Perhaps, as an indication of his belief in humour (and sweet nonsense) as a cultural force, his image of the good Vizier's house is full of fun and kind nonsense. There is no trace of that in Almuene and Fareed. The women, except for the kind Khatoon, from both the houses — the leading ladies and the slave girls — laugh and mock in their respective styles. It is natural for Khatoon to be grave. She lives constantly under the evil spell of Almuene. The farcical hypocrisis of Shaikh Ibrahim, the old superintendent of the Caliph's gardens, in Act IV, Scenes i, ii and iv, contribute to the comic spirit of the play and foreshadow the happy ending. Inspired by Baghdadi wine and the presence of Anice before him, he drops the garb of hypocrisy and sings out the saga of his life:

> When I was a young man,
> I'd a very good plan;
> Every maïd that I met,
> In my lap I would set,

12. Quoted in *Sri Aurobindo — A Biography and a History*, by K.R.S. Iyengar, p. 125.

What mattered her age or her colour?

But now I am old
And the girls they grow cold
And my heartstrings, they ache
At the faces they make,
And my dancing is turned into dolour.[13]

Very deliberately, the playwright suspends his proverbial language skill and finer sense of humour and uses a coarse style, which is ideally suited to the consciousness of the perverted old man. Perhaps, Sri Aurobindo left a clue for the new playwrights that the Shakespearean form and style could still be used in the new age and that drama might move further ahead along the same lines. *The Viziers of Bassora* solves, in its own way, the problem of contemporary speech-rhythm in a Shakespearean framework. Tagore became a successful playwright by largely avoiding the Shakespearean and the classical patterns of drama.

13. Sri Aurobindo, *SABCL*, vol. 7, p. 698.

14

Sri Aurobindo's Rodogune
The Relevance of Tragedy

THE world knows Sri Aurobindo as a great philosopher, *yogi* and an evolutionary thinker, who lived in England from his 7th to 21st year (1879-93) to complete his formal education. The story of his rapid Indianizing from 1893 onwards and his turn to a secluded life of meditation after a stormy political life (1906-08) have fascinated many across the ocean. His life in Pondicherry (1910-50) has also drawn the attention of the elitist Westerner, although his status as a poet and a dramatist has been the point of controversy in India since his quiet passing in December 1950.

Slighted as a poet and a playwright, neglected as some one exercising in "Roget's Thesaurus" (Lal: iv) and a "vast onion of a poem" called *Savitri* (Walsh: 76), Sri Aurobindo is back in focus in the new millennium with the publication of the two-volume *Perspectives* of *Savitri* (Deshpande 2000 and 2002), which have strung together some of the most significant essays on his artistic merit. Today, the average Indian reader has started looking at his poetry with a sense of respect. But then, another line of criticism has gained intensity in the recent past. Books on Indo-Anglian literature streaming into the Indian markets have been bent on proving the uselessness of his plays. Was he really a novice as a playwright? Were the plays not meant for the stage? Are the themes and forms of the plays still relevant? These are some of the questions that float around the corridors of the English departments in India.

I would like to interpret here the deeper intentions of a tragic playwright, for whom the old forms and the old issues were still relevant in a new age. The form was not a return to the past ages in a romantic spirit; it was not a flight from the reality or a distraction from the basics of Sri Aurobindo's views on life, literature and *yoga*. As a versatile literary artist, he was probably thinking of the survival of the tragic form in the twentieth century, and also perhaps of the role of poetry on the new stage. A campaigner for the lyric, Sri Aurobindo was also meditating on the future of drama in his poetic manifesto, *The Future Poetry*:

> Again, it is not likely that the poetic imagination will ever give up the narrative and dramatic form of its creative impulse; a new spirit in poetry, even though primarily lyrical, is moved always to seize upon and do what it can with them — as we see in the impulsion which has driven Maeterlinck, Yeats, Rabindranath to take hold of the dramatic form for self-expression as well as the lyrical spirit of their dominant subjectivity. — *SABCL*, 9, 1972: 7

However, as a practising playwright, Sri Aurobindo was not quite interested in the new spirit in drama, the lyrical and the symbolic pattern, which was the favourite form with Rabindranath Tagore. He seems to have been making a new experiment in tragedy based on the Sophoclean and the Shakespearean models, a blend of the principles of the two giants, who were quite alive to him. He took the pessimistic spirit of Sophocles exercising in the prophecy of doom. And from Shakespeare he learnt the art of varying speech styles to differentiate the various types of consciousness operating behind the characters. The characters of Sri Aurobindo's plays are more or less sensational figures, whom Sri Aurobindo as a spiritual *guru* would have discouraged. Readers familiar with his philosophy will remember his caution against the plane termed "vital," which has been troubling humanity since man's arrival on earth. As a Shakespearean playwright, he cannot afford to offer his views directly on the transformation of the vital nature in Man, which is the zone located between the heart and the sex centre. He can just hint at the better patterns, like *Rodogune*, who are ahead on their way to go out of the sensational trap in their consciousness. I take up *Rodogune* as an instance of the creative spirit of young Aurobindo, who was quite purposefully enlarging the scope of the existing order of tradition as a new playwright. He was using old materials for a new age. His age needed some lessons in true love and sacrifice, some awareness of the futility of vital desires. The society in which young Aurobindo lived needed glimpses of refined aspirations, the finer taste in love and sex. He would also indicate the price of wrong living. He realized that Oedipus and Othello were serious problems for human nature. I would like to present *Rodogune* as an example of his mastery of the old form in a new creative idiom, which he wished to use for a new target audience. The freedom fighters of renascent India were not ideal characters and Sri Aurobindo perhaps wished to make them aware of the value of finer emotions against the backdrop of lust, cruelty, power-politics and ego, which ultimately lead to the tragic end in life.

By the end of the nineteenth century the impression was clear that prose drama was insufficient and poetry was not a luxury but a necessity in the act of drawing out the essence of life. Sri Aurobindo seems to have been contemplating the possible integration of poetry and drama on the modern stage. He must have thought of the double role of poetry, a poetry which conveys both action and emotion at the same time. In *Rodogune,* he takes us back to an old world of kings, queens and intrigues. In doing so, he was not seeking to avoid the contemporary speech style. The rhetoric of the old world quite often comes close to a modern and even post-modern accent, as his figures have been motivated by that universal problem: man's vital nature, which makes Shakespeare and Sophocles so real for us. *Rodogune* is a vital creation by an author who also knows the finer principle of life with the psychic stamp on them. The psychic being is man's soul in evolution from birth to birth. In Sri Aurobindo's philosophy, it means that centre in us, which lies behind the physical, mental and vital being. It is the true plane of man. When the psychic being comes to the front leaving behind the physical, mental and vital beings, then only one begins to lead the true spiritual life. Yet nothing is forced into our comprehension by the creator. It appears throughout as a naturally unfolding drama leading to a tragic end. The Sophoclean and Shakespearean memories in the dialogues are not plagiarism; they are part and parcel of a very powerful allusive style. This is the style that reminds. A desperate Cleopatra, who wishes to suppress the truth that among the twins Antiochus is the older, generates a Sophoclean tension in her effort to influence Mentho, the Egyptian nurse, in favour of the younger twin, Timocles, who impresses her by flattery. But it is also the voice of Sri Aurobindo, a champion of Truth:

CLEOPATRA. Mentho, sit by me, Mentho,
You have not breathed our secret?
Keep it, Mentho, Dead in your bosom,
buy a queen for slave.
MENTHO. Dead! Can truth die? (2.5.391)

The playwright hides his face behind Cleopatra's vital response to Mentho's question and this time it is the transformation of a common Shakespearean moment:

> Ah, Mentho, truth! But truth
> is often terrible. Justice! But was ever
> Justice yet seen upon the earth? man lives
> Because he is not just and real right
> Dwells not with law and custom but for him
> It grows by whose arriving our brief happiness
> Is best assured and grief prohibited
> For a while to mortals. — 2.5.391

Sri Aurobindo wishes to present the image of an unhappy woman in Cleopatra, and the speech is a miracle of exactitude. All of her amoral actions against Antiochus and Rodogune have been caused by her personal frustrations because of an unhappy marriage.

The name of an apparently passive woman in the title, especially when there is a tragic hero in Antiochus, has been a surprise. And it is exactly the point of Sri Aurobindo's newness as a tragic dramatist. For there is an evolution of consciousness in the hero (Antiochus) and the anti-hero (Timocles), which would not have taken place so quickly without the influence of Rodogune upon their lives. The story is a simple tragedy. Cleopatra's twin sons, Antiochus and Timocles, return to Syria after the death of their stepfather the king. Cleopatra wrongfully crowns the junior twin, Timocles, because Antiochus is bold and straightforward like Cordelia and Edgar and refuses to speak that glib and oily art to speak and purpose not. Both the brothers love Rodogune, who chooses Antiochus with a perfect example of unadulterous love. Phayllus, a new variation of Lago, and his sister Cleone, side with Timocles. When Antiochus returns to Syria to save his country by joining hands with Timocles, Phayllus completes the disaster by killing Antiochus with a view to winning Rodogune for Timocles. Rodogune gives her life on the dead body of Antiochus, thereby frustrating Timocles and Phayllus. Timocles recovers his sanity and orders the slaughter of Phayllus and the banishment of Cleone. Now, it is just emptiness and a void for Timocles. Sri Aurobindo wishes to suggest that a man's life becomes meaningful through self-restraint and sacrifice, when he is capable of understanding the need of a fellow human being.

II

What then are the signs of Sri Aurobindo's creative experiment in a world dominated by the consciousness of Oedipus, Hamlet and Othello? The character of Rodogune itself is an original creation. The symbol of rose in the play stands for intensity, passion and delight. The harlot Cleone identities herself with that enchanting flower. Rodogune's image develops as a contrast to the enchantress Cleone. "A floating lily in moonlight was her sister," Eunice hints at her low voltage charm in Act I, Scene I (337). Sri Aurobindo gives us the highlights of Rodogune's physical charm through Eunice, a cousin to the twins and companion of Cleopatra. In Act II, Scene 2, Eunice refers to Rodogune's "blushes," "liquid love-filled eyes," "frightened lashes," "tall dainty grace," "large eyes" and "vague faint pallor just like twilit ivory." Timocles, who lives in the vital, has also been impressed by her dignified charm. His images of Rodogune — "pale goddess," "strange holiness," "deep-hearted miracle," "glorious eyes" — are in harmony with Eunice's, but spoken through the lower vital to flatter her. Rodogune detects this lower vital vibration in Timocles and expresses that exactly to Eunice a little later:

". . . With such wild passion burning under his lids / I never thought to see in human eyes" (2.2.377).

Rodogune is a refined human being, who is not just frank, bold and feminine, but has intelligence and the power to see the deeper things of life. More introspective than Antigone and Rosalind, her shyness in the arms of Antiochus makes her a typical Bengali heroine of the early twentieth century Bengali fiction. The love scenes in the play are more elaborate and sensuously romantic than those that we see in a Shakespearean comedy. The Aurobindonian hero and heroine may be extremely romantic in speech and action even when they feel the approaching steps of doom. Rodogune and Antiochus do not hesitate to enjoy the present moment even though they have an inkling of a dark tomorrow. The same stance appears in the heroes and heroines of *Urvasie* and *Love and Death,* the two long narrative poems written in his early twenties. Death can wait, but not love:

> RODOGUNE. Release me, O release me!
>
> ANTIOCHUS. Not till our lips have joined Eternal
> wedlock. With this stamp and this
> And many more I'll seal thee to
> myself. Eternal Time's too short for
> all the kisses I yearn for from thee, O
> pale loveliness, Dim mystery! Press
> thy lips to mine. Obey. Again! and so
> again and even for ever Chant love,
> O marvel, let thy lips' wild music
> Come faltering from thy heart into my
> bosom.
>
> *Rodogune sinks at his feet*
> *and embraces his knees.* — 2.3.383

Rodogune then rises with an ecstasy, which she cannot control. She hides her face in her hands and Antiochus uncovers her face again. What he says now is a preface to a major theme in Aurobindo's later poetry, a theme which young Aurobindo had been struggling to discover. In fact, Sri Aurobindo spent a lifetime trying to know what it really was. One finds here the foreknowledge of the poet of *Savitri* in Antiochus' speech:

> Hide not thy face from love. The gods in heaven
> Look down on us; let us look up at them
> With fearless eyes of candid joy and tell them
> Not Time nor any of their dooms can move us now.
> The passion of oneness two hearts are this moment
> Denies the steps of death for ever. — 2.3.383

The epic victory of love over death is still an impotent war cry of the passionate heart. It is still a blank prescience yearning towards a future victory. The epic is a dream until now; the tragic is the reality. Death says the final word, but Aurobindo places love above everything else. Rodogune's self-giving indicates she has left the baser self behind her. Her capacity for sacrifice has made her the poet's ultimate choice as a person. It is not hard to see why the play is named after her. Antiochus, too, has a refined glory; he is noble, a true lover and a patriot. But, the playwright exposes his egoistic nature first in a speech in Act I, Scene 2, where he boasts of his "royal nature" and "kingly form" (348) and then in a long soliloquy in Act IV, Scene 4, just before Eremite hints at his impending death. Compared with the *sattvik* nature of Rodogune, Antiochus appears to be *rajasik*. *Sattvik* stands for equilibrium, good, harmony, happiness and light, while *rajasik* expresses struggle and effort, passion and action.

For the first time in tragedy, the leading character possesses no fatal flaw. Rodogune is merely a victim of fate. Then what makes her a tragic character? Perhaps it is her inability to save Antiochus that makes her a heroine of tragedy. Despite her goodness, the element of power is lacking in her nature, the power that saves, the power that can challenge God or the Lord of Death. Sri Aurobindo's later heroine, *Savitri,* has that force, that power of looking straight into the eyes of Death. Passive suffering can well be the subject of tragedy if that is seen as a limitation in the character concerned. In Rodogune, there is no effort to change her fate or the fate of Antiochus; there is no prayer or meditation in her; no effort to grow in the power of God. Yet she has that power to give life at will when her body has become useless in this life, in this manifestation. To love Antiochus is what she was born for. That was her *sadhana* (spiritual practice), her *svadharma* (law of her individual nature). She does not kill herself like a Rajput woman leaping into the fire; she simply leaves her body. For her living is not only torture, it is useless. Much before her death, she had indicated her type in Act III, Scene 2, her *svadharma*:

> God gave my heart and mind; they are not hers
> To force into this vile adultery.
> I am a Parthian princess, of a race
> Who choose one lord and cleave to him for ever
> Through death, through fire, through swords, in hell, in heaven.
> — 3.2.408

Obviously, this is not a hunger of the flesh. In the Aurobindonian vision, this love comes to the human being from God and to God it returns. It is a totally unadulterous or one-pointed love. It is curious how Rodogune is seen here anticipating the speech of Savitri in *The Book of Fate* (Book VI: canto I): "Once my heart chose and chooses not again" (432). But then the epic is beyond the reach of Rodogune. She is tragic; she lacks that Force. Was the playwright searching for that Great Woman who would appear before him later in his life as the "magnet" of man's "difficult ascent" (314)? Was he already thinking of the Great Woman who chased a dark figure beyond the human shores because he was taking away her husband, her truth? Unlike Tagore's, Sri Aurobindo's dramatic characters are always evolving through contrary principles. Timocles constantly swings from bad to good and from good to bad, finally realizing how he has ruined the possibility of his own happiness. When he criticizes Antiochus with the following words — his brother has obstructed his desire — he sees himself in his own rhetoric:

> A despot's sensual longing for a slave,
> Carnal, imperial, harsh, without respect,
> The hunger of the vital self, not raised,
> Refined, uplifted to the yearning heart. — 3.1.410

Sri Aurobindo must be telling us objectively that we are what we see. Except for Rodogune no other character in the play is his extreme favourite. Man is a multiple being. He indicates through Antiochus' speeches how pride lurks behind nobility and how a Timon is going to be trapped by his own awareness of nobility. Antiochus has that characteristic arrogance of Oedipus, though not when he stands before Rodogune. When Eremite says in Act III, Scene 3, that he never shall be king, Sri Aurobindo recreates Oedipus for a modern audience; as if an Indian MP of 2006 is aspiring to be a minister and standing helpless before a soothsayer:

> Who art thou, speak,
> Who barr'st with such ill-omened words my way
> Discouraging new-born victory? What thou know'st,
> Declare! Curb not thy speech. I have a mind
> Strong than omens. — 3.3.415

The greater realism of Sri Aurobindo's plays — a realism that relates him to Shakespeare, and not to Tagore — lies in his ability to see man as a multiple being. Timocles, the Cassanova, whom Rodogune calls an "inconstant moth," (2.2.375) cannot wholly forget his brother's affection for him. He has also an eye on the evil in Phayllus, "I know you love me but your thoughts are evil" (5.1), but he is unable to come out of his spell until the death of Rodogune. Even Cleone, the harlot, sings of the value of youth in Act I, Scene 1:

> Youth, youth! For we shall have upon the throne
> No grey beard longer, but some glorious boy
> Made for delight, with whom we shall be young
> For ever. — 1.1.343

Is it just an anticipation of sensuality for Cleone or Sri Aurobindo's words against the old politicians in the India of 1906? He was extremely critical against the moderates and loyalists, the politicians who were senior leaders of the Indian National Congress.

Rodogune is a permanent aspect of goodness in the play. Antiochus is mellowed by her company and subdues his ego in favour of a true love for his country. He discovers his large self in Act IV, Scene 4, through his love for Rodogune. To indicate the change in him, Sri Aurobindo alludes to the pre-death speeches of Cleopatra in Shakespeare's *Antony and Cleopatra.* Antiochus experiences a feeling of wideness in his self:

> A god! Yes, I have godlike stirrings in me.
> Shall they be bounded by this petty world
> The sea can span? — 4.4.431

In a new creative moment, the playwright has at the back of his mind the inner rhythm and intonation of Shakespeare's Cleopatra who is going to embrace death:

> Give me my robe. Put on my crown. I have
> Immortal longings in me. — 5.2.275-6

Would it be justified then to call Sri Aurobindo an imitator? Certainly, we cannot call an original dramatist a mere replica of the past authors. This is his favourite style of reminder. In *Sri Aurobindo: Seer and Poet* (20-45), V.K. Gokak has examined the allusive style in his poetry. He confirms the intelligent and deliberate creative efforts of Sri Aurobindo. In drama, too, he is a deliberate creator using his allusive style with the same frequency that we see in his poetry. Again and again, we come across either the Shakespearean moments or the Sophoclean situations in fresh contexts. Antiochus' long soliloquy in Act IV, Scene 4, blends the emotion of Antony and Hamlet; first Antony's despair on the eve of his final disaster and then Hamlet's emotional gesture about the mystery of existence. Let us listen to the masterful allusive style of Sri Aurobindo:

> All to night
> Seems strange to me; my wars, ambition, fate
> And what I am and what I might have been,
> Float round me vaguely and withdraw from me
> Like grandiose phantoms in a mist. Who am I?
> When come I? Whither go, or wherefore now?
> Who gave me these gigantic appetites
> That make a banquet of the world? Who set
> These narrow, scornful and exiguous bounds
> To my achievement? O, to die, to pass,
> Nothing achieved but this, "He tried great things,
> Accomplished small one." — 4.4.431-2

Readers familiar with Sri Aurobindo's philosophy will not equate the passage with that typical renaissance introspection. For there is a distinct hint at the gradually expanding self of Antiochus along with some more serious questions relating to the inner voyage of man. Suffering is unmistakably behind this growth. Here is an egoist with a meditative mind. Unlike Rodogune, he has mixed motives: kingdom, power spirituality and Rodogune. But Rodogune has just one central motive:

I have no country, I have only thee.
I shall be where thou art; it is all I know
And all I wish for. — 4.4.430

As a playwright, Sri Aurobindo has something of the Shakespearean power, which helps him present various types of men and women on the stage. What he says of Shakespeare in *The Future Poetry* is also true of his own dramatic style: ". . . his way indeed is not so much the poet himself thinking about life, as life thinking itself out in him through many mouths, in many moods and moments . . ." (*SABCL*, 9: 71-72). As he matured as a prophet of the future, he dropped the dramatic form and concentrated on treatise, lyrics and the epics. But the dramatic power remained with him till the end of his life. Just a single book is a mighty proof of his dramatic genius. That is *Savitri*. One may reject the message of the epic as too futuristic. But, no sensible critic will fail to see its dramatic moments and variety of speech styles.

Drama could not be a lifelong obsession for a poet who was thinking of the transformation of human nature with the help of a supramental ascent and supramental descent. He could speak of such a change only in terms of high poetry, which he did in his mature sonnets, lyrics and *Savitri*. Naturally, he constructed a specific theory of poetry in Pondicherry, but he never attempted to record a theory of his drama. The question naturally arises: why did he write so many plays from 1893 to 1910? And why was the spiritual material so suppressed or oblique in his major plays like *Perseus the Deliverer* (1907), *Rodogune* (1906), *The Viziers of Bassora* (1898), *Vasavadutta* (1915), and *Eric* (1912)? The answer may be traced back to the disturbed social and political conditions of the time he spent in Baroda and Calcutta from 1893 to 1910. It was the time of a great national movement in which he took an active part. On 4 May 1910, he left Calcutta for Pondicherry leaving behind all dramatic tension, the worlds of Shakespeare and Sophocles, in search of a higher spiritual peace and silence. He remained a politician in Pondicherry, but the tension was gone for ever. His Pondicherry phase was the time for the poetry of silence. The drama disappeared from his consciousness and he invited it only occasionally in *Savitri* and *Illion.* However his practice of drama in Baroda and Calcutta had given birth to a very original pattern, where the Shakespearean and the Sophoclean moments had come alive in fresh contexts of despair and doom, love and death.

III

The Shakespearean variety in *Rodogune* needs some elaboration with reference to Sri Aurobindo's philosophy of man as a multiple being, which he began explaining from 1914 onwards in his great prose works, such as *The Life Divine, The Synthesis of Yoga* and some other works serialized in *The Arya,* a monthly philosophical journal. I suspect he had already known the idea in the pre-Pondicherry days. Maybe he had not got enough scope in Baroda or Calcutta to explain the concept of man as a multiple personality. Murari M. Bhattacharya aptly summarizes the issue of man as a multiple creature:

> Our being is not composed of one unit or one stuff: we are far from being single entities, but composed of many entities lurking behind the apparent single one. While one of them aspires for the worthiest, another may abhor it and prefer running after pleasure, notwithstanding its foreknowledge about the evil effect which is sure to follow in the long run. The latter is stronger in us and that is why the aspiration of the former is doomed to end in suppressed sighs and

> unshed tears. Similarly contradictory parts of entities lurk in us which are not in agreement with each other.
>
> — Bhattacharya: 4

In Sri Aurobindo, there is a detailed research into the structure of human consciousness. The great Indian *yogi* has made new discoveries in the human consciousness showing the existence of numerous planes inside us working either separately or in collaboration, fused together at times, often a deeper plane overlapping from behind to be mixed up with a crude surface layer like the lower vital and the physical plane. Because most of the characters in Rodogune are from the vital worlds, one must remember the three layers of the vital: vital proper, the lower vital and the higher vital. In Sri Aurobindo's philosophy, this plane has received a lot of importance. If properly used, the vital or the life-force may be of immense use to man. But an uncontrolled vital misdirects a human being. Timocles and Cleopatra have been governed by the lower vital: passion for power, depression due to obstructed desire and (for Timocles) an unnatural passion for Rodogune. Again, these characters, especially Timocles, are sometimes capable of finer thoughts, which come from the interference of man's true being, whom Sri Aurobindo has called the psychic being. Basically a product of the lower vital, Cleopatra projects her psychic being (at least faintly), where she remembers her two children in Act I, Scene 1:

> Sometimes I think they are not changed at all
> And I shall see my small Antiochus
> With those sweet sunlight curls, his father's curls,
> And eyes in which an infant royalty
> Expressed itself in glances, Timocles
> Holding his brother's hands and toiling to me
> With eyes like flowers wide-opened by the wind
> And rosy lips that laugh towards my breast. — 1.1.339

This is a rare moment in an otherwise vital character. The case of Timocles is very curious but real. Here is a character who is misled by the lower vital, sexuality and power. Yet, again and again, he shows his better self. Sri Aurobindo would have called him Mr Dramatic and Mr Melancholy. Here is Sri Aurobindo's observation on that area of human consciousness:

> . . . the man of sorrows: a fellow . . . covering himself with a sevenfold overcoat of tragedy and gloom and he would not feel his existence justified if he couldn't be colossally miserable. — cited in Satprem: 76

After the death of Rodogune and Antiochus, Timocles moves from drama to melancholy:

> O brother, brother,
> I have sent thee into the darkling shades,
> Myself am barred the way. — 5.5.467

He has never been a villain. Phayllus has misguided him throughout and quite often he has felt the evil in his suggestions. The fact that his love for Rodogune is based on *physicality* does not deny the fact that he is a multiple being. His love for Antiochus peeps in through his crude exterior from time to time and his final speech shows his genuine affection for him, which has been subdued by his surface persona. The inner person comes out in this moving speech. The sense of missing his brother is very authentic here and the sense of nostalgia deepens his isolation. The doctrine of *karma* (we ourselves are our fate through our actions) is very clear in Timocles. While Antiochus too is a vital creation with his strong ego-sense and passion for the throne, he is capable of the higher or finer vital and he has occasional gatepasses to the psychic in his love for his motherland and Rodogune. Besides, one witnesses an evolution of consciousness in

Antiochus. If Timocles is a Shakespearean hero brooding over an error of judgement, Antiochus is Aurobindonian because the departing soul has felt a wideness in his self through his developing inlook into the true mystery of life:

> Break me, I see you can, O god. But you break
> A body, not this soul; for that belongs, I feel,
> To other masters. — 4.4.434

There is always an oblique hint at his maturing self. Sri Aurobindo never brings in the word spirituality or psychic directly. We are just given to understand that Antiochus is growing in depth and purity and that his consciousness is aspiring for higher things. There is a crude violence in Timocles, which is contrasted with the refinement of Antiochus. There is a direct suggestion of a growing sense of the meaning of death in Antiochus:

> What were Death then but wider life than earth
> Can give us in her clayey limits bound?
> Darkness perhaps! There must be light behind. — 5.4.453

He is already sensing the fact that death is a passage to new worlds. Death is close as Phayllus makes the introduction for the executioner, Theras. Phayllus who exploits the lower vital of Timocles reminds us of Iago and Bosola. But, Theras repents instantly as an allusion to Duncan's murder.

> THERAS. Will not this blood stop flowing?
>
> ANTIOCHUS. The blood? Let the gods have it; 'tis
> their portion. — 5.4.456

The killer becomes a chorus. This is an outstanding situation on the stage. The stage direction shows that he meant Rodogune for the stage. The subtlety of the choric device and stage direction relates him to Arthur Miller and Tennessee Williams, especially to the use of lights in the moments of exposure in *Death of a Salesman* and *A Streetcar Named Desire.*

ANTIOCHUS. Tell Parthian Rodogune I wait for her
Behind Death's barrier.

THERAS. The world's too still. Will he not speak
again Upon this other side of
nothingness?
O sounds, sounds, sounds! The
sentries change, I think.
I'll draw thy curtains. O thou mighty
sleeper.

He draws the curtains, extinguishes the light and goes out. All is still for a while, then the door opens again and Eunice and Rodogune enter. — 5.4.456

The sudden change in Theras is quite realistic. That is how a good soul reacts after he or she has done evil. Sri Aurobindo was a master of psychology, as is evident from his major prose works written between 1914 and 1918, like *The Life Divine* and *The Synthesis of Yoga.* He even knew how to use the occult in a tragedy in a convincing way. In the room, where Antiochus lies dead, Rodogune feels a dark presence: "There is some awful presence in this room" (5.4.457). Eunice confirms the presence. Then they discover the corpse. Professor Iyengar sees "a surge of monstrous unnatural behaviour" in the play: "Mother against children and children against mother, brother against brother, daughter against father, even sister against brother, civil strife, brother-murder — all Hell verily let loose" (131). Prema Nandakumar holds an identical view (147).

Rodogune is an exceptionally well-written tragedy both in terms of vision and language and it is difficult to believe that it was written by a young playwright. Unlike Tagore, Sri Aurobindo, the poet, was virtually a late bloomer. But the playwright in Aurobindo had bloomed in his early 1920s, as

The Viziers of Bassora still shines before us as a masterpiece of comic art. It was good for poetry; good for those who would like to see this world becoming God's visible garden house some day! But then, the entry of high poetry meant the exit of the dramatic form. He mastered the art quickly and switched off too soon the channels of Shakespeare and Sophocles, Terence and Aristophanes. It was a great loss for drama. Tagore stuck to the dramatic form till quite late in his life. But, it was a different kind of drama, where subjectivity was a dominant note

Works Cited

Aurobindo, Sri, *Savitri: A Legend and a Symbol,* Pondicherry: Sri Aurobindo Ashram, 1951.

———, *Collected Plays and Short Stories,* Part II, vol. 7, *Sri Aurobindo Birth Centenary Library,* Pondicherry: Sri Aurobindo Ashram Trust, 1972.

———, *The Future Poetry and Letters on Poetry, Literature and Art,* vol. 9, Sri Aurobindo Birth Centenary Library, Pondicherry: Sri Aurobindo Ashram Trust, 1972.

———, *Rodogune, Collected Plays and Short Stories,* Part I, vol. 6, Sri Aurobindo Birth Centenary Library, Pondicherry: Sri Aurobindo Ashram Trust, 1972.

Bhattacharya, Murari M., *Man: A Multiple Personality,* Pondicherry: Sri Aurobindo Society, 1985.

Deshpande, R.Y., ed., *Perspectives of Savitri,* 2 vols., Pondicherry: Aurobharati Trust, 2000 and 2002.

Gokak, V.K., *Sri Aurobindo: Seer and Poet,* New Delhi: Abhinav, 1973.

Iyengar, K.R.S., *Sri Aurobindo: A Biography and a History,* Pondicherry: Sri Aurobindo International Centre of Education, 1972.

Lal, P., ed., *Modern Indian Poetry in English,* Calcutta: Writers Workshop, 1969.

Nandakumar, Prema, "*Rodogune: A Study.*" Sri Aurobindo Circle 23 (1967).

Satprem, *Sri Aurobindo or The Adventure of Consciousness,* tr. from the French by Tehmi, Pondicherry: Sri Aurobindo Ashram Trust,

1968.

Shakespeare, William, *William Shakespeare*: *The Complete Works*, ed. Peter Alexander, London: ELBS, 1965.

Walsh, William, *Readings in Commonwealth Literature*, Oxford: Clarendon, 1973.

15

Two Motives in Poetry
Radha and the Mother

TAGORE either aspires for a female figure or himself becomes a woman in his quest for the Divine. By and large, he has worked in the tradition of *Vaisnava Padavali*, the poetry that had reflected the sense of sweet adoration for Radha or Krishna. Tagore recreates the spirit of *Padavali* for a new audience knowing well that the sense of separation is an eternal human situation. The dark clouds, the rains and the smell of rain-bathed flowers create the same old sensation in our hearts as they did in the hearts of Radha in the Vaisnava Poetry. In Sri Aurobindo's poetry, this Radha consciousness gets a new treatment and ultimately verges on the aesthetics of Mother-worship.

The concept of Mother-worship has never been the central motive in Tagore's prose and poetry. His law of being has always felt comfortable with the essence of Vaisnava aesthetics, upon which he has constructed a new path by fusing beauty and sweetness.

> When I go alone at night to my love-tryst,
> birds do not sing, the wind does not stir, the houses
> on both sides of the street stand silent.
> It is my own anklets that grow loud at every step and I am ashamed.
> When I sit on my balcony and listen for his footsteps,

> leaves do not rustle on the trees, and the water is still
> in the river like the sword on the knees
> of a sentry fallen asleep.
> It is my own heart that beats wildy — I do not know how to quiet it.
>
> When my love comes and sits by my side,
> when my body trembles and my eyelids droop,
> the night darkens, the wind blows out the lamp,
> and the clouds draw veils over the stars.
> It is the jewel at my own breast that shines and gives light. I do not know how to hide it.[1]

Always in such sweet love poems of Tagore, there is a queer assortment of pain and a vague thrill. Sometimes, a strange world is created, which stands between agony and joy.

> I hoped my love would be saved from the shivering shame
> of the shelterless, but you turn your face away.
> Yes your path lies open before you, but you have cut-off my return, and left me stripped naked before the world with its lidless eyes staring night and day.[2]

When Sri Aurobindo translates Nidhu Babu, Chandidas and other Bengali poets, something of this pain is retained from the original texts.

> Now when I've loved thee to my own undoing,
> O marvel ! all my piteous tears and suing
> To bless me with thy presence cannot move thee.[3]

In his original poems, Sri Aurobindo's love for Krishna takes on a new colour. The gesture is totally different in his sonnets and lyrics. There is nothing of the feminine charm of a Chandidas or a Tagore in his sonnet entitled *Krishna*. This

---

1. Sisir Kumar Das, *The English Writings,* vol. I, p. 87.
2. Ibid., p. 110.
3. Sri Aurobindo, *SABCL,* vol. 8, *Translations*, p. 273.

Krishna is the ultimate goal of human aspiration and it is a masculine aspiration, quiet, serene and bold. One easily listens to the new tone:

> At last I find a meaning of soul's birth
> Into this universe terrible and sweet,
> I who have felt the hungry heart of earth,
> Aspiring beyond heaven to Krishna's feet.
>
> I have seen the beauty of immortal eyes.
> And heard the passion of the lover's flute,
> And known a deathless ecstasy's surprise
> And sorrow in my heart for ever mute.
>
> Nearer and nearer now the music draws
> Life shudders with a strange felicity;
> All nature is a wide enamoured pause
> Hoping her lord to touch, to clasp, to be.
>
> For this one moment lived the ages past;
> The world now throbs fulfilled in me at last.[4]

This "Krishna" lies beyond death and pain. The poet's love for him is a quiet and steady flame of aspiration, moving upward through the supermind into the province of everlasting *Sachchidananda*. There is no vital or sensational thrill in the poet's emotion. It is a quiet and noiseless fire, a burning brazier, rising towards the Supreme Divine. Let us have a look at the opening lines of a poem, which is also entitled "Krishna":

> O immense light and thou, O spirit-wide boundless
> Space,
> Whom have you clasped and hid, deathless limbs, gloried
> face?[5]

There is nothing of the sweetness of the Bengali mind imagining the beautiful lord in love. Written between 1936 and 1937 (there

---

4. Sri Aurobindo, *SABCL*, vol. 5, p. 139.
5. Ibid., p. 590.

is just one handwritten draft available in Sri Aurobindo Ashram Archives), this poem speaks of a maturer realization. The poetry is bare and less attractive for the ordinary mind, but this is poetry of a rare experience.

> One is there, Self of self, Soul of Space, Fount of Time,
> Heart of hearts, Mind of minds, He alone sits, sublime.[6]

In Sri Aurobindo's poetry, Krishna is the supreme Divine consciousness; he is the ultimate Divine. He cannot be properly described in terms of language. The ancient Sanskrit poets had recourse to some special linguistic devices, certain words and phrases, to express Him. Sri Aurobindo has to be traditional in translating words like limitless, immeasurable, deathless, etc. But, his expressions have become more concrete because of the evolution of the earth-consciousness since the time of the Vedic and the Upanishadic seers.

Besides, the concept of the World Mother as a mediating force between man and the Divine has also become clearer with the passage of time. Krishna or the supreme Divine has consented to be close to us as the Divine Mother. The ascent to the Krishna-consciousness is a hard passage. It is with the help of the Mother's force that the path to the Lord becomes easy. In Sri Aurobindo's *yoga*, the surrender is to be made to the Divine Mother, who herself does the *sadhana* for the human individual. Just a turning to the Mother means one is registered in her notebook and thereafter it becomes her *sadhana* through the *sadhaka*. Anyone who is turned to the Mother is doing Sri Aurobindo's *yoga*. In fact, very few can get above the sexual impulse without this Mother-worship. Sri Aurobindo stresses on this principle repeatedly in his prose and poetry indicating a marked departure from the sweet Radha-sense of Tagore

---

6. Ibid.

and the Vaisnava poets. Most probably, he believes that the Radha-sense should come only after a great purification in all parts of our being with the direct help of the Divine Mother. The Mother sits at the heart of the Lord and although she is the Radha, Sri Aurobindo wishes us to see her as the Mother until the great transformation takes place in all the parts of our being. There must be a preparation for the ultimate love and only the Divine Mother as the *guru* knows when and how an individual will be ready for the final embrace of Love. Sri Aurobindo has no ambiguity in his Truth-vision. Here are some famous lines from *Savitri*:

> She is the golden bridge, the wonderful fire.
> The luminous heart of the Unknown is she . . .
> She is the Force, the inevitable Word,
> The magnet of our difficult ascent. . . .[7]

This Force is leaning on the earth consciousness and lies very much within our reach. The images, "bridge" and the "magnet," tell all. Humanity has the advantage of both the bridge and the magnet, which make the journey smooth and easy. The magnet is set by Krishna himself. Sri Aurobindo uses the images of the mediator in another text, which sheds light on the Force. The following observation appears at the end of his great little book entitled *The Mother*:

> The power that mediates between the sanction and the call is the presence and power of the Divine Mother. The Mother's power and not any human endeavour and *tapasya* can alone rend the lid and tear the covering and shape the vessel and bring down into this world of obscurity and falsehood and death and suffering Truth and Light and Life Divine and the Immortal's *ananda*.[8]

---

7. Sri Aurobindo, *Savitri: A Legend and a Symbol*, p. 284.
8. Sri Aurobindo, *SABCL*, vol. 25, *The Mother*, pp. 40-41.

Sri Aurobindo repeatedly tells us that the Supermind descent can only be made possible if the mediating Force takes the initiative. His poetry too emphasizes the need of the individual's surrender to the Mother's force. This has created the new aesthetics of Mother-worship in the poetry written in the English language. The ascent to the supreme Godhead is an ascent through the Mother's force. In a poem entitled "The Mother of Dreams," he speaks of this journey beyond the Mother through the Mother:

> Into thy dream-worlds we pass or look in thy magic glass,
> then beyond thee
> we climb out of Space and Time to the peak of divine endeavour.[9]

As contrasted with the sweetness of Bengali poetry, Sri Aurobindo's poetry has a bare strength of direct vision of a supreme Truth-consciousness. This poetry is heroic by virtue of the courage of new explorations in the interior areas of the being and the higher zones of spiritual consciousness.

---

9. Sri Aurobindo *SABCL*, vol. 5, p. 68.

16

Some Notes on the Two Playwrights

Sri Aurobindo's plays contain plenty of action and quite often allude to Sophocles and Shakespeare. Tagore, on the other hand, cuts out a new path in his dramas of ideas, a form completely new in the Indian scene. Yeats and Maeterlinck might have been his models from the Western world, but one searches in vain for an Indian tradition behind Tagore's formal experiments in plays like *Red Oleanders, Achalayatan* (The Immovable Establishment), *Dakghar* (*The Post Office*), and *Raja* (*The King of the Dark Chamber*). The ideas too seem fresh. Such plays come either from a visional romantic or from a poet in revolt against the laws of earth. Tagore, the mystic, is unmistakably present in the plays like *Dakghar* (*The Poet Office*), *Malini* and the *Sannyasi* or *The Ascetic* with his obvious self-projections.

But then, Sri Aurobindo, the mystic, seldom projects his personality in his plays. Quite often in plays like *Rodogune* and *Perseus the Deliverer,* he creates a helpless world of death and doom, even though he has left enough clues in them as to the ascent of man to spiritual heights. Tagore expresses his typical mystic longing in multiple characters within a play, giving us the impression of a one-pointedenss, a lyrical element, which has made all Marlovian heroes author-centric. Sisir Kumar Das reserves two plays — *The King and the Queen* and *Sacrifice* — for the Shakespearean Canon but observes the essential isolation of Tagore, the playwright, from the mainstream theatre.

> He started his career as a playwright at a time when the Bengali theatre was passing through an exciting phase. But he did not write for the public stage nor did he have any connection with it. His self-chosen isolation from the mainstream of theatre gave him a measure of freedom to experiment with forms and themes without compromising with popular taste or the demands of the moneyed proprietors controlling the theatre. But it also strengthened a suspicion about the stage-worthiness of the plays, which were labelled as "poetic" and lacking in "action."[1]

But who knows if he was anticipating a future form of drama cast in the mould of what Sri Aurobindo calls "future poetry"? A change of consciousness — a turning inward in search of the true soul secret — must necessarily call for a new form of drama in the days to come. Multiple characters speaking in the poetic mode could be a hint for the great inwardization, which, according to Sri Aurobindo, will appear in many individuals in a spiritual society of the future. In Tagore's own translations, a refined aspiration wakes up frequently linking him with the poets of *Savitri* and *Prometheus Unbound*. Let us listen to Arjuna's words at the beginning of Scene II in *Chitra:*

> Was I dreaming or was what I saw by the lake truly there? Sitting on the mossy turf, I mused over bygone years in the sloping shadows of the evening, when slowly there came out from the folding darkness of foliage an apparition of beauty in the perfect form of a woman, and stood on a white

---

1. Sisir Kumar Das, ed., 1996, *The English Writings of Rabindranath Tagore*, vol. II, pp. 24-25, Sahitya Akademi, New Delhi.

> slab of stone at the water's brink. It seemed that the heart of the earth must heave in joy under her bare white feet. . . .[2]

This is not exactly the image of Sri Aurobindo's World Mother. But certainly this is Tagore's subjective self in search of a finer beauty, which is caught in the form of a new kind of drama. Not too far from Tagore's lyric voice, such utterances appear again and again through the characters of his plays. In Scene VII, another character named Vasanta utters the same idiom reflecting authentically the lyric voice of the born romantic:

> The loveliness of your body will return tomorrow to the inexhaustible stores of the spring. The ruddy tint of thy lips freed from the memory of Arjuna's kisses, will bud anew as a pair of fresh *asoka* leaves, and the soft, white glow of thy skin will be born again in a hundred fragrant jasmine flowers.[3]

This may be dramatic weakness, but this is the authentic Tagore, the playwright. He cannot variate the speech styles, which express the emotional centres. The *sannyasi* in *The Ascetic* caught by the charms of an evening twilight speaks once again the authentic idiom of the great lyricist.

> The gold of the evening is melting in the heart of the blue sea. The forest, on the hillside, is drinking the last cup of the daylight. On the left, the village huts are seen through the trees with their evening lamps lighted, like a veiled mother watching by her sleeping children. Nature, thou art my slave, thou hast spread thy many-coloured carpet in the great hall where I sit alone, like a king, and watch thee dance with thy starry necklace twinkling on thy breast.[4]

---

2. Ibid., pp. 39-40.
3. Ibid., p. 47.
4. Ibid., p. 64.

The *sannyasi*'s return to earth is another way of expressing the Aurobindonian love for this earth. The tone and the voice are not Aurobindonian, but typically Tagorean. There is another difference. Sri Aurobindo never speaks of this return journey in his plays; he speaks about this only in his lyrics, sonnets and *Savitri*. But then, it is curious how Tagore echoes the Aurobindonian idea in a half-conscious spiritual gesture.

> The bird flies in the sky, not to fly away into the emptiness, but to come back again to this great earth — I am free. I am free from the bodiless chain of the Nay. I am free among things, and forms and purpose. The finite is the true infinite, and love knows its truth.[5]

Although Tagore is referring here to a very mundane love, the basic idea is the same, as all loves basically contain the principles of the psychic and spiritual love, which we see in Sri Aurobindo's cosmic epic as the flaming love of the *Mahashakti* or the World Mother for this suffering earth. Let us listen to Savitri's speech in the Epilogue, where she addresses Satyavan, the symbol of the earth, and explains the necessity of the mundane life.

> We have borne identity with the Supreme
> And known his meaning in our mortal lives.
> Our love has grown greater by that mighty touch
> And learnt its heavenly significance, yet nothing is lost of mortal's love's delight.
> Heaven's touch fulfils but cancels not our earth. . . .[6]

Tagore and Sri Aurobindo have strongly spoken against asceticism. While Sri Aurobindo conceals his personal stance in his plays, Tagore projects his own views against asceticism

5. Ibid., p. 67.

6. Sri Aurobindo, 1951, *Savitri: A Legend and a Symbol*, p. 341, Sri Aurobindo Ashram, Pondicherry.

both in his poetry and plays. The lyric voice of Tagore comes out in the open in the closing pages of *The Ascetic*.

The subjective voice is basically a mellow female voice on a numberless occasion, be it from the mouth of a male or a female figure. It appears naturally through the mouth of Malini echoing quite often the persona of the *Gitanjali* poet. Let us listen to the very opening speech in *Malini,* which Malini utters:

> The moment has come for me, and my life, like the dew drop upon a lotus leaf, is trembling upon the heart of this great time. I shut my eyes and seem to hear the tumult of the sky, and there is an anguish in my heart, I know not for what.[7]

The voice of the *Gitanjali* poet cannot be mistaken:

> The day is no more. The shadow is upon the earth. It is time that I go to the stream to fill my pitcher.
> The evening air is eager with the sad music of the water. Ah, it calls me out into the dust. In the lonely lane there is no passer by, the wind is up, the ripples are rampant in the river. I know not if I shall come back home. I know not whom I shall chance to meet. There at the fording in the little boat, the unknown man plays upon his lute.[8]

There is that typical vague thrill about meeting somebody in a sudden moment of Grace. Tagore is unable to conceal this central aspiration of a spiritual seeker even when the occasions are not apparently spiritual. Throughout the play, Malini echoes the mystic language of her creator, who is steeped in the spirit of the *Vaisnava Padavali*. There is very little interaction of speeches, as we can see in the following exchanges. The brahmanas are just forming a chorus to highlight the longing of Malini.

---

7. Sisir Kumar Das, ed., 1996, *The English Writings,* vol. II, p. 73.
8. Ibid., vol. I, p. 68.

Malini. I was born in a king's house, never once looking out from my window. I had heard that it was a sorrowing world — the world out of my reach. But I did not know where it felt its pain. Teach me to find this out.

First brahmana. Your sweet voice brings tears to our eyes.

Malini. The moon has just come out of those clouds. Great peace is in the sky. It seems to gather all the world in its arms, under the fold of one vast moonlight. There goes the road, losing itself among the solemn trees with their still shadows. There are the houses and there is the temple; the river bank in the distance looks dim and desolate. I seem to have come down, like a sudden shower from a cloud of dreams, into this world of men, by the roadside.

First brahmana. You are the divine soul of this world.[9]

Between the romantic girl and the brahmanas, there is virtually no interaction. Obviously, Tagore is aiming at a different kind of dramatic form. Sometimes, two or three characters are allowed to use the lyric voice, as in *The Waterfall.*

Sanjay. Cannot you see the picture of an infinite sorrow in the twilight glow, clinging to that purple hill?

Abhijit. Yes, my heart fills with tears. I never boast of harshness as heroic. Look at that tiny bird, sitting on the topmost branch of the pine tree, all alone. I do not know whether it will go to its nest, or take its journey across the night to a distant forest; but

9. Sisir Kumar Das, ed., 1996, vol. II, p. 77.

> the sight of that lonely bird gazing at the last ray of the setting sun fills my heart with a sadness which is sweet. How beautiful is this world ! Here is my salutation to all that has made my life sweet.[10]

Once again it reads like a subjective lyric from the great Bengali poet, who himself has recreated *The Waterfall* in the English language.

There is another kind of treatment in *Red Oleanders,* where speeches and action bear more interpenetration within a symbolic texture. The woman here, Nandini, is not the image of the World Mother in a direct sense. But then, she is the symbol of life in a mechanized world of collective tyranny. She is love in a dry world. Ranjan, her soul mate, is also the symbol of life. But, life is at stake. There is a cruel king, who does not appreciate life and leisure, love and beauty. Ranjan and Nandini, like Shelley's Asia and Prometheus, are the United Two in search of life in a mechanical world. Ranjan and Nandini produce the impression of a colour, which is red like the red oleanders. The colour stands for life and intensity. Again, it is the intensity of Tagore's own voice that we hear in Nandini's speeches. In a rare moment, Nandini's speech becomes dramatic as she recollects before Bishu the interaction of speeches between her and the king. The whole drama is contained in one single speech, which is loaded with a conflict of ideas.

Bishu. Then what did he say?

Nandini. Starting up and fixing his spear-point gaze on my face, he suddenly said: "I want to know you." I felt a shiver run down my body and asked: "What is there to know? — I am not a manuscript!"
"I know all there is in manuscripts," said he, "but I don't know you."

---

10. Ibid., p. 179.

> Then he became excited and cried: "Tell me all about Ranjan. Tell me how you love him."
>
> I talked on: "I love Ranjan as the rudder in the water might love the sail in the sky, answering its rhythm of wind in the rhythm of waves."[11]

The duel of words becomes sharper after that with a quick fire round.

> All of a sudden, he startled me by exclaiming: "Could you die or him?"
> "This very moment," I replied.
> "Never," he roared, as if in anger.
> "Yes, I could," I repeated.
> "What good would that do you?"
> "I don't know," said I.[12]

This shows that Tagore could very well tackle the traditional form. He just did not wish to follow the known track. His eyes were perhaps focused on a different kind of drama.

In the first chapter of *The Future Poetry*, Sri Aurobindo draws our attention to the new kind of drama associated with mystic poetry in the lyrical form:

> . . . it is not likely that the poetic imagination will ever give up the narrative and dramatic form of its creative impulse; a new spirit in poetry, even though primarily lyrical, is moved always to seize upon and do what it can with them — as we see in the impulsion which has driven Maeterlinck, Yeats, Rabindranath to take hold of the dramatic form for self-expression as well as the lyrical in spite of their dominant subjectivity. We may perhaps think that this was not the proper form for their spirit, that they cannot get there a full or a lawless success; but who shall lay down rules for

---

11. Ibid., p. 228.

12. Ibid.

> creative genius or say what it shall or shall not attempt? It follows its own course and makes its own shaping experiments. And it is interesting to speculate whether the new spirit in poetry will take and use with modifications the old dramatic and narrative forms, as did Rabindranath in his earlier dramatic attempts, or quite transform them to its own ends, as he has attempted in his later work.[13]

Sri Aurobindo wrote *The Future Poetry* between 1917 and 1920 and as such he might be thinking of *The Post Office* (written in 1912); it was translated in 1914 by Devabrata Mukherjee as a "later work." The translation by Mukherjee has not been approved of by many, but somehow it has a kind of lyrical flavour within its natural speech style. *The Post Office* exemplifies the inward turn in drama. The structure of the play and the speeches form an interesting symbolic texture. Unlike the hazy ideas in Maeterlinck's plays, the mystic symbolism in *The Post Office* shapes out smoothly. Interpretations may vary, but the basic idea of the quest for the beyond is unmistakable.

Amal is sick and confined to his room. He has a passion for the sky and far-away provinces. As the curdseller passes by his house, he is fascinated by the tune of his call and yearns to be his companion in a long walk, with the yoke on his shoulder. Yeats was right when he wrote in the Preface to the Macmillan edition: "The deliverance sought and won by the dying child is the same deliverance which rose before his imagination."[14] Amal, the mystic poet in the nursery class, imagines the entire journey of the curdseller: a man walking the long, long road, moving across the river and over the hills

13. Sri Aurobindo, *SABCL*, vol. 9, p. 7.
14. Preface to *The Post Office*, Macmillan Pocket Tagore Edition, Madras, 1986.

and the red road, and then into the village under the big trees. The inward journey is suggested with the help of a natural dialogue between Madhav and Amal.

> Madhav: And where will you go ?
>
> Amal: Oh, I will walk on, crossing so many streams, wading through water.
> Everybody will be asleep with their doors shut in the heat of the day and I will tramp on and on seeking work far, very far.[15]

The dialogue between Amal and the Dairyman is another example of the fusion of natural speech and poetry, poetry which speaks of an indefinable thrill.

> Dairyman: Dear, dear, teach you the tune: what a notion!
>
> Amal: Please do. I love to hear it. I can't tell you how queer I feel when I hear you cry out from the bend of that road, through the line of those trees! Do you know I feel like that when I hear the shrill cry of kites from almost the end of the sky?[16]

It is nameless movement in Amal's heart. When he says, "I seem to feel homesick when I hear you call from far down the road,"[17] the word "homesick" sounds like a blank foreknowledge, a half-conscious memory of the future.

Somehow Tagore has mixed up this quest for the beyond with Death, which is eagerly coveted. Amal's frequent references to the king and his call and his letter have an obvious symbolic function. In this king symbolism, there is a memory of "the Prince of this world" (John 14: 30). The king, the

15. Ibid., p. 35.
16. Ibid., p. 42.
17. Ibid., p. 38.

watchman tells Amal, "sends tiny notes to little boys."[18] Tagore might be remembering here his own boyhood, when he could hear the voice of the Divine. Like mystic poetry, the drama is playing hide-and-seek with the Reality. The play is neither a spiritual drama, nor a "borderline" romance. Sri Aurobindo would have related Amal's emotion to "a blank prescience" that yearns "towards distant change."[19] The playwright sees things through the boy's lens and makes him suffer from half-thought.

Nature is wisdom; Nature opens our eyes to strange things. Early in the play, Tagore ironises the eyeless scholar through Madhav's words — "Early and late they toil and moil at their books, and they've eyes for nothing else."[20] When Madhav wishes Amal to be such a bookworm, the little boy is taken aghast. He refuses to be learned:

Amal:	No, I would rather go about and see everything that there is.
Madhav:	Listen to that! See! What will you see, what is there so much to see?
Amal:	See that far-away hill from our window — I often long to go beyond those hills and right away.[21]

Without life-sense, without the touch of Nature, without a feeling for the book of life, none can "become." For Sri Aurobindo, too, this becoming is the ultimate value of life. Amal, the inexperienced boy, has a faint awareness of this idea. He has left his doors and windows open to let the many-splendoured world in.

18. Ibid., p. 49.
19. Sri Aurobindo, 1951, *Savitri: A Legend and a Symbol*, p. 2.
20. *The Post Office*, p. 31.
21. Ibid., p. 32.

The soul rising from sleep sees and perceives and while the bookworm stoops over the printed words, Amal walks on crossing many streams. The names, Sudha, Badal and Sarat are symbolic of different aspects of Nature. Sudha is expressive of all the glories of Nature; she promises to bring flowers. Badal, the cloud, and Sarat, the season of autumn, are two faces of Nature. They are messages of joy and sorrow, which the postmen usually bring for us.

Amal's passion for the beyond becomes more intense in Act II. "But the day I am well off I go with the *fakir*, and nothing in sea or mountain or torrent shall stand in my way."[22] He visualizes the footsteps of the king's postman walking down the hills alone. It is poetry dressed in prose: the lantern at night, the waterfall changing to a stream at the foot of the mountain, the fields of rye and sugarcane, the snipe wagging their tails and their bills dipped in the mud. These are just paints done with the help of words. He makes us see. In a significant speech Amal appears to be a bit restless. This restlessness is followed by a kind of fear.

> Say, *fakir*. I've been feeling a sort of darkness coming over my eyes since the morning. Everything seems like a dream. I long to be quiet. I don't feel like talking at all. Won't the king's letter come? Suppose this room melts away all on a sudden . . .[23]

This is the fear of leaving without seeing the King's face. The fear passes away and Amal starts feeling well again. He has grown a love for the unknown king. Love has brought contentment. "I feel very well, Doctor, very well. All pain is

---

22. Ibid., p. 70.
23. Ibid., p. 80.

gone. How fresh and open! I can see all the stars now twinkling from the other side of the dark."[24]

Death is peaceful, eventless. All the characters form the chorus. The oil lamp is blown out and the starlight streams in. Sudha is Grace. She brings in the flowers for the departing soul.

24. Ibid., p. 88.

17

The Hungry Stones and The Phantom Hour

Idylls of the Occult

SRI Aurobindo handled the narrative masterfully, not just in his epics and the poetic tales like *Urvasie, Love and Death* and *Baji Prabhou.* He also made casual experiments with the short story, showing his class in those leisurely exercises. It is a misfortune for us that just a single story entitled *The Phantom Hour* has been found in its complete form, from the *inventio* down to the peroration. Three other stories — *The Door at Abelard, The Devil's Mastiff* and *The Golden Bird* — could not survive the onslaught of white ants.

There is a distant memory of Poe's tales in *The Phantom Hour,* although it is quite Aurobindonian in its substance and attitude to life. Tagore was a regular short story writer and he was also fond of the occult and the supernatural. A study of *The Phantom Hour* and Tagore's *The Hungry Stones* will show the interest of the two authors in things supernatural.

The Hungry Stones uses double narrative. The authorial narrator meets a man in the waiting room of a railway station and makes him tell the story of a strange palace. The romantic in Tagore is in love with the past, the scintillating past when "jets of rose water spurted from its fountains" and young Persian women sat on the marble floors of the spray-cooled rooms. Tagore imagines their dishevelled hair before their bath and the splashing sound of their mellow feet in the fresh water of the reservoirs. There is a delicate touch of pain as the second narrator speaks of the lost fountains and the songs and the white feet, which had once pressed the snowy marbles. The author listens without interrupting and the man goes on with his weird story. The descriptions of the river Susta sinking low, its sandy bed and glistening water and the sun sinking behind the hills pull us to the place of action. Unlike the mystic suggestions in *The Phantom Hour,* Tagore's story concentrates on a thrilling flashback:

> As I sat down again, thinking it to be an illusion, I heard many footfalls, as if a large number of persons were rushing down the steps. A strange thrill of delight, slightly tinged with fear, passed through my frame, and though there was not a figure before my eyes, I thought I saw a bevy of joyous maidens coming down the steps to bathe in the Susta in that summer evening. Not a sound was in the valley, in the river, or in the palace, to break the silence, but I distinctly heard the maidens' gay and mirthful laugh, like the gurgle of a spring gushing forth in a hundred cascades, as they ran past me, in quick playful pursuit of each other, towards the river without noticing me at all. As they were invisible to me, so was I, as it were, invisible to them. The river was perfectly calm, but I felt that still, shallow and clear waters were stirred suddenly by the splash of many an arm jingling with bracelets, that the girls laughed and dashed and spattered water at one another, that the feet of the fair shimmers tossed the tiny waves up in showers of pearl.[1]

Such are the lovely descriptions of Tagore in a tale of mystery. The story is not frightening except for some brief moments, and the other world is presented in terms of beauty. The

1. Rabindranath Tagore, *The Hungry Stones and Other Stories*, Rupa and Co., New Delhi, 2002, pp. 5-6.

second narrator is drawn to the palace again and again, mentally and physically, because of its mysterious beauty. The crazy Meher Ali's cry, "Stand apart! Everything is false," goes on mystifying the scenes from the past. As the train comes in, there is no more time for the conclusion. It is time now for the author to conclude with his remarks on the story.

Sri Aurobindo's story creates the willing suspension of disbelief. There is more of action and drama in a Victorian setting. He gives shape to a modern story with London as its convincing background and links the occult and the real like a masterful storyteller. There is no scope inside this action-narrative for a detailed leisurely description of Nature, which we see in Tagore's famous story. The plot in *The Phantom Hour* unfolds naturally through the eyes of the omniscient narrator.

Sturge Maynard, while reading a mystic text describing occult happenings, sees the apparition of a clock indicating the time when his girlfriend Renée will be facing danger. He reaches her place just at eight — following the indication from the ghost clock — and kills her ex-boyfriend just when the man is going to kill Renée. The night is extremely foggy in London and they remove the corpse easily with the help of Renée's maid, Rachel. Sri Aurobindo stresses the idea of fate, which was on their side this time, unlike the case of the previous life, when it had gone wrong for Sturge. The writer is dealing with very vital things in the story. Just a piece of dialogue will reveal how the trekker of the supermind still knows the vital aspects of life, as much as Shakespeare knows them. It is the speech of Renée Idalie's ex-boyfriend:

> I give you still a chance, Idalie — always, always a chance. Will you go with me? You have been false to me, false with your body, false with your heart. But, I'll forgive. I forgive your desertion, I'll forgive this too. Come with me, Idalie.

> And if not, — Renée Idalie Marviranne, it is going to strike eight, and when the hour has done striking, I strike.[2]

Sturge's indifference to Renée's past speaks of the awakened psychic being in him. Through his interior monologue, Sri Aurobindo establishes his theory of rebirth in fiction. There is also that famous apophthegm from the Master's mature world-view, "There is no such thing in this creation as chance,"[3] which we see in the interior monologue of Sturge just before the end of the story. This story alone will prove Sri Aurobindo's mastery of weaving the dialogue and the narrative. While the dialogues are both real and symbolic, the key word "fog" hinting at God's favour to Sturge and Renée, comes back repeatedly both in the narrative and the speeches and monologues. Inside this action-packed story, there are moments of wonder, which are quite usual in the writer of *The Hungry Stones*. Let us listen to that:

> Sturge Maynard rose and waited for some more definite sign. For he divined now that some extraordinary mental state, some unforgettable experience was upon him. His expectation was not deceived. Once more the chimes rang out, this time it seemed to him as if a woman's voice were crying to him passionately under cover of that perfectly familiar melody.[4]

As in *The Hungry Stones,* it is a voice floating back to Sturge from a past life.

> That day again at dead of night I heard the stifled heart-breaking sobs of someone — as if below the bed, below the

---

2. Sri Aurobindo, *SABCL,* vol. 7, *Collcted Plays and Other Stories*, p. 1021
3. Ibid., p. 1024.
4. Ibid., p. 1016.

> floor, below the stony foundation of that gigantic palace from the depths of a dark damp grave, a voice piteously cried and implored me: "Oh, rescue me!"[5]

Unlike Tagore, Sri Aurobindo asserts the authenticity of occult visions and happening. While Sri Aurobindo's excellence lies in the slow unfolding of a dramatic plot, Tagore's wonderful lyricism seizes us throughout his story.

5. Rabindranath Tagore, *The Hungry Stones and Other Stories*, Rupa and Co., New Delhi, 2002, p. 18.

18

Man and the New Species

LIKE Sri Aurobindo, Tagore is aware that man has within him a clue to the Life Divine. Man can remove the problems of disharmony, which are caused by his egoistic impulses and his selfish desires. Our narrow self-conceals our true identity. The discovery of our true being thrills us and the whole world becomes our own. The very essence of soul is unity. In love, the disharmony disappears. For Tagore, love is the highest bliss for man, which makes him realize that he is wider than himself. Love relates him to the universe.

Both the authors know that ego and love do not go together. While Tagore rubs in a little too much with the word sin, Sri Aurobindo excludes the idea from his theory and practice of *yoga*. Let us listen to Tagore:

> For in sin man takes part with the finite against the infinite that is in him. It is the defeat of his soul by his self. It is a perilously losing game, in which man stakes his all to gain a part. Sin is the blurring of truth which clouds the purity of our consciousness.[1]

The Upanishadic idea of sin is not unknown to Sri Aurobindo. But, somehow he is not too fond of the word "sin." He says it in his own idiom:

---

1. Sisir Kumar Das (ed.), *The English writings*, vol. II, p. 73.

> An occasional sinking of the consciousness happens to everybody. The causes are various, some touch from outside, something not yet changed or not sufficiently changed in the vital, especially the lower vital, some inertia or obscurity rising from the physical parts of nature.[2]

The science of the new *yoga* excludes the word "sin" from its vocabulary. In this matter at least, Tagore is more tied to the old texts than Sri Aurobindo. The discovery of the planes of the being in very clear terms is Sri Aurobindo's original contribution to yogic culture. He prefers the word "error." And even error is a possibility for the prophet of the Life Divine.

> In our world error is continually the handmaid and pathfinder of Truth; for error is really a half-truth that stumbles because of its limitations; often it is Truth that wears a disguise in order to arrive unobserved near to its goal.[3]

The progressive enlightenment can only be hastened if man consents to change his nature. The transformation of human nature is not an overnight affair. Sri Aurobindo maps the hitherto unknown planes of human consciousness and shows in detail the ways to transform them with the direct help of that mediating force whom he and Sri Ramakrishna call the Mother. Tagore does not show any interest in the Mother-cult, although here and there in his poems the suppressed feeling for the World-Mother creeps in. In Tagore's book entitled *Sadhana,* we find a general survey of the cosmic consciousness and oneness. The details about those realizations are missing in his prose. In his songs and lyrics, there are

2. Sri Aurobindo, *Bases of Yoga,* Sri Aurbindo Ashram, Pondicherry, p. 49.
3. Sri Aurobindo, *SABCL,* vol. 18, p. 12.

moments of revelation. In Sri Aurobindo's prose and poetry, the experiential ideas are more prolific and the doctrine is always supported by the yogic vision. Moreover, Sri Aurobindo does not stick to a past doctrine; he wishes to reshape the doctrine in the light of the present and the future. However, it is really interesting to see how inspiringly Tagore remembers his tradition in an acquired language.

> Through all the diversities of the world the one in us is threading its course towards the one in all; this is its nature and this is its joy. But by that devious path it could never reach its goal if it had not a light of its own by which it could catch in a flash the sight of what it was seeking. The vision of the Supreme One in our soul is a direct and immediate intuition, not based on any ratiocination or demonstration at all. Our eyes naturally see an object as a whole, not by breaking it up into parts, but by bringing all the parts together into a unity with ourselves.[4]

Tagore means "revelation" here. He does not use the word, which means direct sight; Sri Aurobindo would have called it "a flame throw from identity."[5] Tagore, within his limitations, has a perception of the idea of the Divine's manifestation in common things.

> The touch of an infinite mystery passes over the trivial and the familiar, making it break out into ineffable music. The trees and the stars and the blue hills appear to us as symbols acting with a meaning which can never be uttered in words.[6]

Like Sri Aurobindo, Tagore believes in the ultimate value of man: to find the One, which is in him. The ultimate value of man is that great becoming, when life itself becomes a beautiful

---

4. *The English Writings*, p, 295.
5. Sri Aurobindo, *Savitri*, Pondicherry, 1954, p. 341.
6. Sisir Kumar Das (ed.), *The English Writings*, vol. II, p. 297.

piece of art. The discovery of the One in us removes all contradictions of life. Disharmonies disappear. Work, knowledge and love are harmonized.

> . . . pleasure and pain become one in beauty, enjoyment and renunciation equal in goodness; the breach between the finite and the infinite fills with love and overflows; every moment carries its message of the eternal: the formless appears to us in the form of the flower, of the fruit; the boundless takes us up in his arms as a father and walks by our side as a friend. It is only the soul, the one in man which by its very nature can overcome all limits, and finds its affinity with the Supreme One.[7]

This is what Sri Aurobindo calls "the realization of the All in the individual by the transformation of the limited ego into a conscious centre of the divine unity and freedom."[8] Tagore does not speak about the difference between the mind and the Supermind. Sri Aurobindo clarifies the distinction and tells us how the mind is incapable of achieving or initiating this unity or oneness.

> The principle of unity is above in the Supermind: for there alone is the conscious unity of all diversities; there alone Consciousness and Force arrive at their divine equation.[9]

However, Tagore echoes Sri Aurobindo's idea of man's awareness of his parts and there is a deliberate effort in him to arrive at a harmony of his mind, life and body. Sri Aurobindo sees it as a harmony of man's knowledge and will and emotion, a harmony of all his members.[10] Also, both are

---

7. Ibid.
8. Sri Aurobindo, *SABCL,* vol. 18, p, 59.
9. Ibid., p. 215.
10. Sri Aurobindo.

aware of man's intense conflict with the external world and his wish to search for the principles of harmony. Tagore has an inkling of the divine life on earth; Sri Aurobindo builds the bridge marrying the soil to the sky.

Both in Tagore's prose and poetry, there are very obvious flashes of spiritual thoughts, which form the basis of Sri Aurobindo's major works. I would like to call them Aurobindonian thoughts, because they are the basics and the essentials in the dreamer of *The Life Divine.* While in Tagore, a chameleon and a butterfly, they are just a few among his endless discoveries. Certainly, they are permanent beliefs in the life of an aesthete with an intuitive eye, which opens quite often to the deeper mysteries of life and the eternal law.

> Spiritual life is the emancipation of consciousness. Through it we find immediate response of soul everywhere. Before we attain this life, we see men through the medium of self-interest, prejudice or classification, because of the perpetual remoteness around us which we cannot cross over. When the veil is removed, we not only see the fleeting forms of the world, but come close to its eternal being, which is ineffable beauty.[11]

This sounds a bit bookish with its strong memory of the scriptures. But, quite often the experiential stuff may be seen in exciting metaphorical modes:

> Existence is the play of the fountain of immortality. Wash your soul with its water, you who are old, and feel that you are of the same age with the flower that has blossomed this morning and with this light which carries fresh in its countenance the first smile of creation. This is freedom,

---

11. Sisir Kumar Das (ed.), *The English Writings of Rabindranath Tagore*, vol. III, p. 49.

> freedom from the mist which for the time being masks our spirit with the semblance of blurred age, hiding from us the truth that we are the children of the immortal. Could the child bring such a joy to the heart of man if age and death were true? Does not that joy come from direct recognition of the truth of deathless life, of endless growth and ever-renewed hope of perfection?[12]

Tagore was about 60 when he wrote this and the other passages I am going to refer in this chapter. The passage cited above speaks of Tagore's awareness of a new concept of youth and evolution. While obviously influenced by the Upanishadic concept, Tagore has virtually used the idiom of Sri Aurobindo in the last interrogative sentence. By 1920 Sri Aurobindo had already got a clue to the immortality of life. Also, his theory of evolution accepts the fact that perfection is not an end-stopped stage of consciousness. The soul runs continuously after the ever progressive new. But where does the journey end? What is the map? What are the details of the track and the destination? Sri Aurobindo gives a concrete shape to Tagore's idea of perfection. Like Tagore, Sri Aurobindo knows that all birth is a progressive self-finding, a means of self-realization. However, he knows a little more than the older poet.

> To grow in knowledge, in power, in delight, love and oneness, towards the infinite light, capacity and bliss of spiritual existence, to universalize ourselves till we are one with all being, and to exceed constantly our present limited self till it opens fully to the transcendence in which the universal lives and to base upon it all our becoming, that is

12. Ibid., p. 45.

> the full evolution of what now lies darkly wrapped or works half-evolved in Nature.[13]

Tagore thinks it out in a different style just because he is on the borderline of spiritual consciousness. His is the style of a mystic, because he is not a spiritualist proper. And yet to the common intelligence, Tagore is more attractive than Sri Aurobindo when he talks of man's gradually expanding self.

> Man truly lives in the life that is beyond him; he toils for the unknown master; he stores for the unborn, he leaves the best of his life for reapers who have not yet come; the time which is yet to be is truer to him than the time which is. Man offers himself as a sacrifice for all that lies in the future — all this shows that man is not yet born, his history is the history of birth-throes. Our greatest men bring in their life the message of man's future birth; for they dwell in the time to come, making it ready for ourselves.[14]

Apart from his assured sense of the evolutionary drive in man, Tagore seems to have been struggling to comprehend the greatest value of man. It is not quite certain in the above passage, and yet he seems to have been moving around half-consciously that particular purpose of man, which the Mother has highlighted in a significant prayer, dated 29 August 1914:

> Man is the link between what must be and what is; he is the footbridge thrown across the abyss, he is the great cross-shaped X, the quaternary connecting link. His true domicile, the effective seat of his consciousness should be in the intermediary world at the meeting-point of the four arms of the cross, just where all the infinitude of the Unthinkable

13. Sri Aurobindo, *The Supramental Manifestations, SABCL,* vol. 16, pp. 243-44.
14. Sisir Kumar Das (ed.), *The English Writings of Rabindranath Tagore,* vol. III, p. 46.

> comes to take a precise form so that it may be projected into the innumerable manifestation.[15]

Man is the connector, the blessed species with a marvellous capacity for extension. He is destined to play a major role in creating a new species out of himself. Sri Aurobindo observes:

> Man's greatness is not in what he is, but in what he makes possible. His glory is that he is the closed place and secret workshop of a living labour in which supermanhood is being made ready by a divine Craftsman. But he is admitted too to a yet greater greatness and it is this that, allowed to be unlike the lower creation, he is partly an artisan of this divine change; his conscious assent, his consecrated will and participation are needed that into his body may descend the glory that will replace him. His aspiration is earth's call to the supramental creator.[16]

What Tagore sees half-consciously in terms of poetry, two anthropologists from Pondicherry see it as an inevitable future. But, is it always half-conscious? Sometimes, Tagore knows too clearly that man is a transitional creature and that he is not an end-product in Nature's lab. Let us see how Tagore expresses the idea:

> Man has a feeling that in him the creative manifestation of life has come to the end of a cycle, ready to ascend to one still wider and higher. When life first evolved its physical senses from the depth of amorphous darkness, it came to a wondrous world of forms, and this adventurous spirit of life is yet urging the spirit within man to develop an inner vision which will lead him through these endless forms

---

15. The Mothers, *Prayers and Meditations*, CWM, vol. I, p. 232.
16. Sri Aurobindo, *SABCL*, vol. 17, *The Hour of God*, p. 9.

> into a world of infinite meaning, where he will cross the boundaries of the senses to a freedom which is ineffable.[17]

It is an interesting passage because the poet seems to have known here the laws of science to some extent. It is perhaps wrong to think that Tagore was influenced by Sri Aurobindo around 1920, when the evolutionary philosopher had almost completed his major treatises on the divine life. There is very little similarity between their English expressions. Unlike Radhakrishnan, Tagore was an original philosopher and was too proud about his originality. Copying was against Tagore's nature and even if he had seen some essays in *The Arya,* he had seen them as a creative writer. Besides, he had known other evolutionary philosophers and had believed in them through his experiential knowledge.

---

17. Sisir Kumar Das (ed.), *The English Writings of Rabindranath Tagore,* vol. III, p. 69.

19

Tagore and Sri Aurobindo on Modern Poetry

BOTH the authors seem to have suspected the terms "modern," "modernism" and "modernity." They were also not quite enthusiastic about modern poetry. While Tagore reacted with a sharp sophisticated sarcasm in his essay entitled *Modern Poetry* (a translation by Indira Devi Chaudhurani from Bengali), Sri Aurobindo was cool and disinterested when he wrote back to his disciples responding to their queries. Both of them expressed their views in the 1930s, when post-modernistic qualities were already creeping into the world of poetry and putting a kind of pressure on them. Sri Aurobindo was not a public figure and as such he was less bothered about the changing fashions in the province of poetry. For him, poetry was either beautiful or inferior. He never characterized it as ancient or modern, except for some general references to "ancient" and "modern" poetry, as we see in Chapter IV of *The Future Poetry.* He must have disliked the interference of intellect in the poetry of the 1920s, 1930s and 1940s. But then, he stayed behind the curtain with his supreme confidence and belief that contemporary reputation was a fluke.

Tagore reacted more nervously and angrily, because of the distinct rise of post-modernism (it was mistakenly known as modernism till the 1970s), which challenged his position and threatened to put a back-dated label on his high class poetry. Bishnu Dey, Buddhadeva Bose, Achintya Kumar Sengupta and a few others were pushing him hard. The essay on *Modern Poetry* (1932) seems to have been an exercise in self-defence. The tone and implied gesture at the start cannot be overlooked;

> Who defines the modern age in terms of the almanac?[1]

For Tagore, any twist or turn in literature is modern. He recollects that the pre-Romantics and the Romantics like Wordsworth, Shelley, Keats, Coleridge and Byron were known as modern poets in his boyhood.

> An individual's measure of delight was, in those days, the sign of modernism. Wordsworth expressed in his own style the spirit of delight that he had realized in Nature. Shelley's was a Platonic contemplation to which he had added a spirit of revolt against every kind of obstacle, political, religious or otherwise. Keats' poetry was wrought out of the meditation and creation of beauty. In that age, the stream of poetry took a turn from outwardness to the inwardness.[2]

Tagore's argument is quite clear and convincing. In the nineteenth-century England, modernism meant subjectivism or self-expression. The poets and writers of the 1920s and the 1930s did not wish to cling to that romantic mode. T.S. Eliot's *The Waste Land* (1922) was a turning point. Tagore ironically refers to himself as an "old-fashioned" poet contrasting with the stark realists:

> Science has thoroughly examined every pulse beat, and declares that at the root of things there is no illusion; there is only carbon and nitrogen, there is physiology and

---

1. Sisirkumar Ghose, ed., *Angel of Surplus: Some Essays and Address on Aesthetics*, Visva-Bharati, Calcutta, 1978, p. 112.
2. Ibid., p. 112.

> psychology. We old-fashioned poets thought that the illusion was the main thing and carbon and physiology the by-products. We must confess that we had striven to compete with the Creator in spreading the snare of illusion through our rhyme and rhythm, language and style. In our metaphors and nuances there was an element of hide-and-seek: we were loath to lift aside that veil of modesty which adorns and does not contradict truth. In the coloured light that filtered through the haze, the dawns and evenings appeared in a beauty as tender as a bride. The modern violent realists, engaged in publicly disrobing beauty, is a sight we are not accustomed to.[3]

With this Tagore adds three questions, which I would like to stress, simply because they indicate the disturbed existence of a famous poet and shed light on his artistic stance. "Is it merely habit that makes us so uncomfortable; is there no truth is this sense of shame? Does not Beauty become bankrupt when divested of the veil which reveals rather than conceals?"[4] The "personal man" in Tagore raises his voice against a dark aspect of science; it does not select in terms of the person, his need of the immaterial and his vision. Science does not care for building the ties of relationship:

> It does not regard what "I" want as the main consideration, but rather what the thing in itself exactly is, leaving "me" out of the question. And without "me" the need for illusion is over.[5]

Many have mistaken this glorification of the "I" in Tagore for sheer egoism. Far from that, it is quite in harmony with Sri Aurobindo's spiritual existentialism, which refuses to erase

---

3. Ibid., p. 113.
4. Ibid.
5. Ibid., p. 114.

the personal consciousness of the *yogi*. The glorious "I" of Sri Aurobino's sonnets is an evolution of the Tagorean "I".

Both Tagore and Sri Aurobindo were aware of the quality of restraint and economy in the poetry of the post-1920s. In a letter, Sri Aurobindo disclaims his authority on the subject, but understands "that the turn there is to suppress emotion, rhetoric, colouring, sentiment and arrive at something very direct, expressive, recording either the thing exactly as it is or some intimate essential truth of the thing without wrapping it up in ideas and sentiments, superfluous images and epithets."[6] He reminds us — he has also spoken of another trend in his days in the last few chapters of *The Future Poetry* — that this is not the only sign in the poetry of his times.

> It does not look as if all contemporary English poetry was like that, it is only one strong trend; but such as it is, it has not as yet produced anything very decisive, great or successful. Much of it seems to be mere flat objectivity or, what is worse, an exaggerated emphatic objectivity; emotion seems often to be replaced by an intensified vital-physical sensation of the object.[7]

Sri Aurobindo's opinion virtually supports the views of Tagore expressed in his *Modern Poetry*. Just a year before the publication of Tagore's essay, Sri Aurobindo had observed and cautioned in a letter:

> I admit I have not read as much of "modern" (contemporary) poetry as I should have — but the little I have is mostly of the same fundamental quality. It is very carefully written and versified, often recherché in thought and expression; it lacks only two things, the inspired phrase and inevitable

---

6. Sri Aurobindo, *SABCL*, vol. 9, p. 441.
7. Ibid., p. 441.

> word and the rhythm that keeps a poem forever alive. Speech carefully studied and made as perfect as it can be without reaching to inspiration, verse as good as verse can be without rising to inspired rhythm — there seem to be an extraordinary number of poets writing like this in England now. . . . It is not the irregular verses or rhymes that matter, one can make perfection out of irregularity — it is that they write their poetry from the cultured striving mind, not from the elemental soul-power within. Not a principle to accept or a method to imitate![8]

Tagore's tone is different from Sri Aurobindo's. As the makers of modern Indian tradition, the two culture heroes seem to have been quick to feel the limitations of modern poetry. Tagore was more sarcastic. He was a public poet from the romantic school proper. That is precisely the reason behind his sarcastic reaction. It was a threat to his poetic fame:

> In the process of economizing that is being carried out in the poetry of this scientific age any kind of adornment has become taboo. A fastidious selection in the matter of rhyme, rhythm and words has become almost obsolete. The change has been far from gentle, for in order to break the spell of the past it has become the fashion to repudiate it aggressively. It has been something like trying to arrange bits of broken glass in an ugly manner. A modern poet writes: "I am the greatest laughter of all, greater than the sun, than the oak tree, than the frog and Appollo." "Than the frog and Apollo" is where the bits of broken glass come in, lest someone might think that the poet is arranging his words prettily. If the word "sea" were used instead of "frog" the modernists might object to it as regular poetizing. That may be so, but the mention of the frog is also poetizing, of an opposing kind. That is to say, it is not introduced naturally but is like

---

8. Ibid.

> someone deliberately walking on your toes. That would be merely modern.[9]

The romantic in Tagore disapproves of the post-modern blend of the ugly and the beautiful, especially when the ugly is unnaturally placed by the pretty. The so-called impersonality in modern or post-modern poetry comes in for criticism. Also, looking at life as a whole is not a new phenomenon in poetry. Therefore, Tagore refuses to accept it as a modern element. He goes back to Li-Po, a Chinese poet who wrote more than a thousand years ago, and sees the same detachment and wholeness. The old poets could see things dispassionately. Quite relevantly, Tagore refers to some examples from Li-Po. Let us have a look at the first two to verify Tagore's logic:

> Why do I live among the green mountains?
> I laugh and answer not, my soul is serene;
> It dwells in another heaven and earth belonging to no man,
> The peach trees are in flower, and the water flows on.[10]
>
> Blue water . . . a clear moon . . .
> In the moonlight the white herons are flying.
> Listen! Do you hear the girls who gather water-chestnuts?
> They are going home in the night, singing.[11]

The observations have little of the decorative stuff, which the modern poet hates. Tagore was also trying to show the magic of simplicity and the deeper sense lying beyond that apparently transparent exterior. In translation, Li-Po's lines are well up to our age. Antique or modern, poetry has to be beautiful — that is Sri Aurobindo's stance. Labels are useless; they do not mean much. Sri Aurobindo refuses to part with

9. Sisirkumar Ghose, ed., *Angel of Surplus*, pp. 114-15.
10. Ibid., p. 119.
11. Ibid., pp. 119-20.

rhythm for the sake of a new trend. Rhythm is a necessity, not a luxury. In Chapter IV of *The Future Poetry,* while making a general reference to "ancient" and "modern" poetry, he asserts the value of rhythm:

> Rhythm is the premier necessity of poetical expression because it is the sound movement which carries on its wave the thought-movement in the word; and it is the musical sound-image which most helps to fill in, to extend, subtilize and deepen the thought impression or the emotional or vital impression and to carry the sense beyond itself into an expression of the intellectually inexpressible — always the peculiar power of music. This truth was better understood on the whole or at least more consistently felt by the ancients than by the modern mind and ear, perhaps because they were more in the habit of singing, chanting or intoning their poetry while we are content to read ours, a habit which brings out the intellectual and emotional element, but unduly depresses the rhythmic value. On the other hand modern poetry has achieved a far greater subtlety, fineness and depth of suggestion in style and thought than the ancients, — with perhaps some loss in power, height and simple largeness.[12]

This passage written between 1917 and 1920 probably meant by "modern" the poetry since the 1890s. It shows a kind of balance between the "ancient" and "modern" poetry, an equal respect for the "modern" by which he probably meant the poetry written between 1890 and 1917 at least, excluding poets like Yeats and Whitman, who cared very much for rhythm. But, in his letters written in the 1930s, he was distinctly critical about the lack of rhythm in what may be called post-modern poetry. He was still using the term "modern" for "post-

---

12. Sri Aurobindo, *SABCL,* vol. 9, p. 23.

modern" poetry. The term matters little in this case. In a letter written around 1932, he was thinking of Yeats and A.E. George Russell as the survivors in a new age, showing his unhappy awareness of the "latest craze" in England:

> The latest craze in England is either for intellectual quintessence or sensations of life, while any emotional and ideal element in poetry is considered as a deadly sin. But beautiful poetry remains beautiful poetry even if it is not in the current style. And after all, Yeats and A.E. are still there in spite of this new fashion of the last one or two decades.[13]

He obviously meant "post-modernism" without using the term. His silence on T.S. Eliot only confirms his indifference to post-modernism in poetry. Unlike Tagore, Sri Aurobindo was not entirely dismissive. He was less ironical than Tagore and more balanced in his letters written in the 1930s and 1940s. He accepted the fact that it was a new way of looking at things in poetry and saw the trend as an effort to see things directly and precisely. He was also quite tolerant of experiments, constructive in his comments and careful to detect the exact problems. Let us conclude the chapter with such a passage of constructive criticism, which we do not really see in Tagore's essay on modern poetry:

> On the road that is being now followed there is also evident danger of decadence, through an excess of mere technique and artifice or through a straining towards the merely out-

---

13. Ibid., p. 444.

> of-the-way or the perverse. But there seems to be no other door of progress than to make the endeavour.[14]

For Sri Aurobindo, the right endeavour in poetry is to shun the surfaces and move inward to investigate into the interior zones of the being. There are other trends in modern poetry, apart from surface realism, which he observes with curiosity, like mysticism and surrealism, impressionism and symbolism.

---

14. Ibid., p. 443.

    See also *Kallole* by Goutam Bhattacharya, *Papyrus,* Calcutta, 1987, for a detailed picture of the Non-Rabindrian Movements beginning clearly from 1923 and gaining in intensity by the beginning of 1930. Tagore's sarcastic essay on Modern Poetry came out in 1932.

20

Two Kinds of English Prose

I

It is now easy to judge the English writings of Rabindranath Tagore, because the three volumes from Sahitya Akademi are before us. The cultured Bengali has not been quite appreciative of Tagore's English, which, he says, is not English. It is an insult to one of the greatest writers of non-fiction from the Indo-Anglian school. It is true that Tagore's English is not as smooth as Sri Aurobindo's or Nehru's, but who can deny the great thoughts behind his English, which he expresses in his own peculiar way? In the context of globalization of the English language, Tagore's Bengali-flavoured English has to be valued in its own right.

The point is: his English reads well and takes inspired leaps frequently. There are moments when he suffers from vagueness, but even his vagueness puts on a mystic colour and has a sweeping impact on the readers. When he expresses the idea of new mysticism, which has no contradiction with Matter, he has his own style. Here is a beautiful passage:

> To be able to love material things, to clothe them with tender grace, and yet not to be attached to them, this is a great service. Providence expects that we should make this world our own, and not live in it as though it were a rented tenement. We can only make it our own by some service, and that service is to lend it love and beauty from our soul.

> From your own experience you can see the difference between the beautiful, the tender, the hospitable and the mechanically neat and monotonously useful.[1]

There is a superfluity in this passage, which is due to a Bengali way of thinking. The Bengali is a feminine language. Only Vivekananda could change its character. Tagore enchants us with his ornamental Bengali. And it is this tendency, which has affected his English. Now let us see how Sri Aurobindo uses the language.

> Mastery of the material does not mean having plenty and profusely throwing it out or spoiling it as fast as it comes or faster. Mastery implies in it the right and careful utilization of things and also a self-control in their use.[2]

In his prose Sri Aurobindo uses poetry only when it is a necessity. Tagore can seldom check his poetry in prose and quite often it is a very Bengali poetry that he is translating into English.

> When all my thoughts were furiously revolving, like dead leaves, in a whirlwind of desire for raising funds, a picture came to my hand.[3]

Yet there are wonderful aphorisms by Tagore in very smart and catchy English. They bear the memory of an Emerson or a Thoreau, but they are unmistakably Tagorean. Around 1920, his English expressions reached the acme of perfection, especially in his maxims.

---

1. Sisir Kumar Das ed., *The English Writings of Rabindranath Tagore*, vol. III, p. 61.
2. Sri Aurobindo, *Bases of Yoga*, Sri Aurobindo Ashram, Pondicherry, 2001, p. 65.
3. Sisir Kumar Das ed., *The English Writings*, vol. III, p. 271.

> The sign of greatness in great geniuses is their enormous capacity to borrow, very often without their knowing it; they have an unlimited credit in the world market of culture. Only mediocrities are ashamed and afraid of borrowing, for they do not know how to pay back their debt in their own coin. Even the most foolish of critics does not dare blame Shakespeare for what he openly appropriated from outside his own national inheritance. The human soul is proud of its comprehensive sensitiveness; it claims its freedom of entry everywhere when it is fully alive and awake.[4]

Tagore is virtually echoing Eliot's attitude to tradition and creativity. But the language is his own and the last sentence is the best. It shows Tagore's mastery of the wisdom style even in an acquired tongue. The critic of language will find a slip here and a jarring note there. But can he deny the expressive quality in Tagore's English? Can he deny the originality of his thought? He does not write like Sri Aurobindo or K.D. Sethna. But, he writes well, sometimes very well. Of course, there are moments of dullness in his English prose, moments when he is fascinated by the graceless words like "rudimentary," "unobstructive," "appraisement" and "apportionment." Those are moments, perhaps, when he is thinking out a Bengali word or idiom and then searching for its English equivalent.

II

Buddhadeva Bose's remarkable essay on Tagore's Bengali prose may be read as a relevant commentary on his English prose too, even though Bose has not touched on the issue of his English prose. What he says of Tagore's Bengali prose is in many ways applicable to his English prose. In a skilful summary, Bose draws our attention to the general complaints against his Bengali prose.

4. Ibid., p. 71.

> Tagore's repetitions are far from few, his tangential passages are numerous, he uses imagery rather than reasons, and metaphors rather than facts; he starts with the professed intention of proving a thesis and ends by sharpening our perceptions; where an intellectual debate is expected he makes the illicit move of producing enchantment.[5]

Bose corroborates the view, but goes on to see the outstanding features of Tagore's prose. In a way, the same limitations — if one really calls them limitations — may be found in his English non-fictional prose. However, the rational critical judgement does not quite illumine always the real strength of an intuitive prose writer. Tagore is more poetic than Sri Aurobindo in his non-fiction, but that does not really degrade the quality of Tagore's prose. There may remain logic in a great poetic-prose; in the hands of superior artists poetry itself becomes logic of superior accuracy. Sri Aurobindo blends poetry and logic wonderfully in *Essays on the Gita*, just because he knows the power of an intuitivised logic, which rises far above the mere intellectual gymnastics. Tagore, too, has his own characteristic method in his Bengali flavoured English prose, where long drawn-out metaphors offend the intellectual critic. But, we have to judge him as he is, and should not be disappointed because he does not write like Russell or Sri Aurobindo.

Buddhadeva Bose turns a bit irrelevant when he says, "No one can deny that Tagore is not even a critic, in the sense that Aristotle or Anandavardhana is one."[6] Why should we expect him to copy the past classical masters, especially when he is a romantic critic having a fresh pair of eyes? He has his own

---

5. *A Centenary Volume*: Rabindranath Tagore: 1861-1961, Sahitya Akademi, New Delhi, 1961, p. 102.

6. Ibid.

system. Let us cite a passage from his Preface to *Sadhana*, where he speaks of the existence of another kind of critic.

> The meaning of the living words that come out of the experiences of great hearts can never be exhausted by any one system of logical interpretation. They have to be endlessly explained by the commentaries of individual lives, and they gain an added mystery in each new revelation. To the verses to the Upanishads and the teachings of Buddha have ever been things of the spirit, and therefore endowed with boundless vital growth; and I have used them, both in my own life and in my preaching, as being instinct with individual meaning for me, as for others, and awaiting for their confirmation, my own special testimony, which must have its value because of its individuality.[7]

This is the new critic's art of self-defence. After reading this, we cannot deny him the title of the "critic." He is a critic in his own right and his criticism is often complementary to Sri Aurobindo's views on art and aesthetics. All his writings on the relation between the individual and the universe have been densely metaphorical and poetic in essence, but one must be sympathetic and patient enough to see how he clarifies his viewpoints within the texture of his superabundant prose. Like Sri Aurobindo he stresses the value of expanding the human consciousness. There is no haziness about his English when he puts his emphasis on this issue:

> When a man begins to have an extended vision of his true self, when he realizes that he is much more than at present he seems to be, he begins to get conscious of his moral nature. Then he grows aware of that which he is yet to be. . . . [8]

---

7. Sisir Kumar Das ed., *The English Writings*, vol. II, p. 278.
8. Sisir Kumar Das ed., *The English Writings*, vol. III, p. 68.

The larger life depends on the expansion of man's consciousness. This is just the essence of the basic Aurobindonian philosophy, which also includes a system of expansion through the *yoga* of transformation or integral *yoga*. Personal aggrandizement makes us small and imprisons us within the dark boundary walls of the limited ego. The discipline required is the preparation for thinking of the other, our brother man. We have to share the burden of our fellow beings. We have to give away to gain something. To expand gradually the consciousness of one's unity with all is the striving of humanity. This is just the echo of the Sri Aurobindonian aspiration for integrated living. Both Tagore and Sri Aurobindo have criticized the isolation of the world-leaving monks. The point is: we have to be here amidst the crowd and change the consciousness of the multitude by changing our individual consciousness. The clue to this true living was not known to the ancient monks; only the *rishi*s knew it well. The *rishi*s accepted all life and sought to go beyond life with the help of life. The Divine has to be realized in this life, not by rejecting life. The rejection of life is the rejection of the Divine. Nature, family and society are there for us to realize the world conscious in all. The arguments of Tagore bear the stamp of his personality even when he is shunning the poetic mode. Again, the poetic mode has a kind of logic, which the common rationality cannot appreciate. This may be called the logic of the intuition. The flower is a message from the Divine, just as the ring from Rama is the authentic identification mark for Sita. There is a typical Bengali sensibility in the following English passage, as if Tagore is translating his characteristic Bengali prose.

> Such a messenger is a flower from our great lover. Surrounded with the pomp and pageantry of worldliness,

> which may be likened to Ravana's golden city, we still live in exile, while the insolent spirit of worldly prosperity tempts us with allurements and claims us as its bride. In the meantime the flower comes across with a message from the other shore, and whispers in our ears, "I am come. He has sent me. I am a messenger of the beautiful, the one whose soul is the bliss of love. This island of isolation has been bridged over by him, and he has not forgotten thee, and will rescue thee even now. He will draw thee unto him and make thee his own. The illusion will not hold thee in thralldom for ever."[9]

There is a feminine quality attributed to a masculine language. Words like "shore" and "whispers" bring back the memories of the *Gitanjali* poems. The idea of living "in exile" is a favourite symbol in Tagore, the mystic poet, who goes on emphasizing the idiom of a romantic mystic with more familiar phrases like "message from the other shore," "whispers in our ears," and "island of isolation." Some of the words create a jarring note in an otherwise beautiful passage. They are "worldliness," "allurements" and "thralldom." The image of "exile" goes well with the word "rescue" torwards the close of the passage. The "flower" is Grace. Only Grace can rescue and initiate the exile's return home. How many English authors have this force of substance? How many take care to achieve this metaphorical unity? If first class English excludes everything inferior to Shakespeare, Milton and Sri Aurobindo, then of course it is another matter. But then, we have to consider the charms and expressive elements in a writer using an acquired tongue. Very few writers have shown us the harmony between the Upanishads and aesthetics, perhaps none better than Tagore and Sri Aurobindo. Unlike Sri

9. Sisir Kumar Das ed., *The English Writings*, vol. II, p. 319.

Aurobindo, Tagore takes up the issue frequently, as if it is an engaging theme in his prose.

> The Upanishads have said that all things are created and sustained by an infinite joy. To realize this principle of creation we have to start with a division — the division into the beautiful and the non-beautiful. Then the apprehension of beauty has to come to us with a vigorous blow to awaken our consciousness from its primitive lethargy, and it attains its object by the urgency of the contrast. Therefore our first acquaintance with beauty is in her dress of motley colours, that affects us with its stripes and feathers, nay, with its disfigurements. But as our acquaintance ripens, the apparent discords are resolved into modulations of rhythm. At first, we detach beauty from its surroundings, we hold it apart from the rest, but at the end we realize its harmony with all. Then the music of beauty has no more need of exciting us with loud noise; it renounces violence, and appeals to our heart with the truth that it is meekness that inherits the earth.[10]

Apart from a slight grammatical uncertainty in the final clause of the passage, it is a wonderful commentary on the link between the Upanishads and aesthetics. The charm of Tagore's English non-fiction lies also in the sudden shifting of the mode from the objective to the subjective, from an impersonal expository passage to a sudden lyricism. Tagore concludes his essay "The Realization of Beauty" with a purely mystic lyric.

> Last night, in the silence which pervaded the darkness, I stood alone and heard the voice of the singer of eternal melodies. When I went to sleep I closed my eyes with this last thought in my mind, that even when I remain

10. Ibid., pp. 334-35.

> unconscious in slumber the dance of life will still go on in the hushed arena of my sleeping body, keeping step with the stars. The heart will throb, the blood will leap in the veins, and the millions of living atoms of my body will vibrate in tune with the note of the harp string that thrills at the touch of the master.[11]

Once again, the prose is a memory of a well-known lyric from *Gitanjali*, although the themes are different.

> I know that the day will come when my sight of this earth shall be lost and life will take its leave in silence, drawing the last curtain over my eyes.
>
> Yet stars will watch at night, and morning rise as before, and hours heave like sea waves casting up pleasures and pain.[12]

In moments of such realizations, Sri Aurobindo maintains his impersonality in his prose and conceals his "I" to express a cosmic feeling. Prose then invites poetry to stand behind it. The Divine speaks through the medium, Himself taking up the pen to express Himself. Here is such a wonderful passage from Sri Aurobindo's commentary on the *Ishavasyopanishad*:

> Lift your eyes towards the Sun; he is there in that wonderful heart of life and light and splendour. Watch at night the innumerable constellations glittering like so many solemn watch fires of Eternal in the limitless silence which is no void but throbs with the presence of a single calm and tremendous existence; see there Orion with his sword and belt shining as he shone to the Aryan fathers ten thousand years ago at the beginning of the Aryan era; Sirus in his splendour, Lyra sailing billions of miles away in the Ocean of space. Remember that these innumerable worlds, most of them mightier than our own, are whirling with indescribable

---

11. Ibid., p. 337.
12. Sisir Kumar Das ed., *The English Writings*, vol. II, p. 74.

> speed at the back of that Ancient of Days whither none but He knoweth, and yet that are a million times more ancient than your Himalaya, more steady than the roots of your hills and shall so remain until He at His will shakes them off like withered leaves from the eternal tree of the Universe. Imagine the endlessness of Time, realize the boundlessness of Space; and then remember that when these are not, He shall be still the same; perceive that beyond Lyra He is and far away in Space where the stars of the Southern Cross cannot be seen, still He is there. And then come back to the Earth and realize who this He is. He is quite near to you. See yonder old man who near you crouching and bent, with his stick. Do you realize that it is God who is passing? There a child runs laughing in the sunlight. Can you hear Him in that laughter? Nay, He is nearer still to you. He is in you. He is you. If is yourself that bums yonder millions of miles away in the infinite reaches of Space, that walks with confident steps on the tumbling billows of the ethereal sea; it is you who have set the stars in their places and woven the necklace of the suns not with hands but by that *yoga*, that silent actionless impersonal will which has set you here today listening to yourself in me.[13]

This vast rhythmic sweep is beyond the scope of Tagore; one really is in doubt about the species who wrote this prose: a man or a new species? Tagore is close to us with his marvellons sweetness, with his pain-tinged romance. His charming incapacities give a new aura and colour to his prose. I have referred to Sri Aurobindo's passage just to differentiate between the two levels of poetry, the poetry of greatness and the poetry of sweetness, which have contributed to the glory in the prose of the two Indo-English writers. The logical texture in Tagore's English prose is remarkably strong in many passages in *Creative Unity*. Quite often he is precise. The

13. *Sri Aurobindo, SABCL,* vol. 12, p. 475.

substance is highlighted and the form limits itself to its proper work of expression with precision. Here is a characteristic passage:

> Poetry and the arts cherish in them the profound faith of man in the unity of his being with all existence, the fine truth of which is the truth of personality. It is a religion directly apprehended, and not a system of metaphysics to be analysed and argued. We know in our personal experience what our creations are and we instinctively know through it what creation around us means.[14]

Although it lacks the flamboyance of Oscar Wilde or Bertrand Russell, it is simply great English prose by virtue of the force and originality of its substance. There are people who keep complaining about Tagore's English, but my citations will speak of the class of Tagore as an English prose writer. Instances may be offered in abundance from anywhere from *Creative Unity, Personality* and *Sadhana*. It is hard to believe one man having no formal education can write English like this. Besides, sincerity and expressive power are certainly more precious than cleverness and empty flamboyance.

III

Sri Aurobindo's non-fiction may be ranked with the works of the great prose masters like Carlyle, Newman, Ruskin, Russell and others. Unfortunately, most people outside India still know him for his prose epic, *The Life Divine*, which is just one of his five masterpieces. The others are *Essays on the Gita, The Synthesis of Yoga, The Human Cycle* and *The Future Poetry*. There are yet other precious gems like *The Ideal of Human Unity, War and Self-Determination. The Foundations of Indian Culture, The Secret of the Veda, The Upanishads* and of course the sparkling letters,

14. Sisir Kumar Das ed., *The English Writings*, vol. II, p. 499.

which have already occupied three fat volumes. V.K. Gokak's words on the letters speak of Sri Aurobindo's class:

> The master plays with an idea or image, word or sound: refutes current estimates; corrects by an Olympian glance critical misapprehensions; takes us through numerous ways to the primordial source of song. He lets fall casually, in two or three letters a whole body of aesthetics. An angelic humour flashes across the letters like gentle lightning now and then and the style is almost always limpid and crystalline, its lyric beauty contrasting sweetly with the architectural and epic grandeur of his major prose.[15]

The great letters were written between 1926 and 1950, at the peak of his maturity, and there was an unusual clarity of syntax and thought in those mature letters. The great Aurobindonian period had started in 1914. He had been serializing then his great prose works in a journal called *The Arya*. He had started writing most of his great works simultaneously and each of them in a new style. *The Life Divine* had been the most complicated. Long afterwards, it was reviewed in the *Times Literary Supplement.* Sisirkumar Ghose has rightly referred to the key observation of the T.L.S. reviewer: "He writes as though he were standing among the stars, with the constellations for companions."[16] Not just in *The Life Divine,* but in all other great prose works, he writes from a conscious height of superiority with a queer gesture of aloofness. Be it the letters or the complicated edifices of the *Arya,* he writes with remarkable ease and smoothness.

---

15. V. K. Gokak, *Sri Aurobindo: Seer and Poet,* Abhinav Publications, New Delhi, 1972, pp. 150-51.

16. Sisirkumar Ghose, *The Poetry of Sri Aurobindo,* Chatuskone Pvt. Ltd., Kolkata, 1969, p. 36.

For over six decades — from 1892 to 1950 — Sri Aurobindo made daring experiments in English prose. He wished to globalize the language by blending the Indian and the European myths, by infusing the intonation of Sanskrit verse into the English syntax and by expressing the subtleties of spirituality in an acceptable variety of English. He was not a butterfly like Tagore, who moved freely on various topics. He stuck to one single theme — the quest for a new species beyond man — and expressed that in different styles. Of course, he expressed the subtleties of new spirituality, the various layers of consciousness, the lower and the higher hemispheres, the psychic opening leading to spiritual ascents, the crossing of the mental zones, the gradations of the plane beyond mind or the Supermind structures, and the essence of *Sachchidananda*. There was also the full scheme of the new *yoga,* which embraces all the areas of life. And there was a detailed analysis of a new theory of poetry as *mantra* in his *The Future Poetry* (1917-21) and in the letters written after 1926.

If his poetry was the poetry of *yoga,* his prose was also the prose of *yoga.* Experiential thought or vision is his basic substance, both in poetry and prose.

> A guidance, a governance begins from within which exposes every movement to the light of truth, repels what is false, obscure, opposed to the divine realization: every region of the being, every nook and corner of it, every movement, formation, direction, inclination of thought, will, emotion, sensation, action, reaction, motive, disposition, propensity, desire, habit of the conscious or subconscious physical, even the most concealed, camouflaged, mute, recondite, is lighted up with the unerring psychic light, their confusions dissipated, their tangles disentangled, their obscurities, deceptions, self-deceptions precisely indicated and removed;

> all is purified, set right, the whole nature harmonized, moulded in the psychic key, put in spiritual order.[17]

Unlike Tagore's prose, this comes directly from yogic experience. Every word speaks of a specialized knowledge. The quality of inspiration is also different as is evident in the breath-stopping flow of single word parallelism.

---

17. Sri Aurobindo, *SABCL*, vol. 19, pp. 907-08.

Conclusion

TAGORE has captured for us the colourful worlds of borderline romance, which stand at the gateway of true spirituality. Restless to a degree, he pines for the far away infinite and seeks to bring the Supreme down to the earth with the help of his extraordinary mental perception of the Divine. His language moves like the dancing damsels of heaven to entrap the Divine in his net of music. He is an embodiment of sweetness and leaves the Vaisnavaa poets far behind in his musical verse of mellow sensitivity. Besides, he has a prescience of the worlds Sri Aurobindo has explored. The foretaste of true spirituality has been imaged in a charming Bengali language, which is his own creation.

Be it poetry or prose, Tagore has either echoed the great Aurobindonian perceptions or imaged the foreknowledge in musical words.

> Man's abiding happiness is not in getting anything but in giving himself up to what is greater than himself, to ideas which are larger than his individual life, the idea of his country, of humanity, of God.[1]

Sri Aurobindo has said the same thing again and again in his *Bande Mataram* editorials. Later in his life, we see him expressing it more masterfully in *The Synthesis of Yoga*. Tagore's

---

1. Sisir Kumar Das, ed., *The English Writings of Rabindranath Tagore*, Sahitya Akademi, New Delhi, vol. II, p. 340.

prescient perception of the true nature of sacrifice becomes more expressive and detailed in the hands of Sri Aurobindo.

> This pure wideness is brought into the intensity of the sacrifice of love when into all our activities there is poured the spirit and power of a divine infinite joy and the whole atmosphere of our life is suffused with an engrossing adoration of the One who is the All and the Highest. For then does the sacrifice of love attain its utter perfection when, offered to the Divine All, it becomes integral, catholic and boundless and when, uplifted to the Supreme, it ceases to be weak, superficial and transient movement men call love and becomes a pure and grand and deep uniting *ananda*.[2]

The idea of expansion is a reality in both the writers, though the experience of Sri Aurobindo is deeper. Call it surrender or sacrifice, expansion or love, Tagore's expressive gestures have a strange appeal to the common humanity. As if he is busy forming a bridge to move across to the higher worlds of Sri Aurobindo's vision.

> I have kissed this world with my eyes and my limbs; I have wrapt it within my heart in numberless folds.; I have flooded its days and nights with thoughts till the world and my life have grown one, — and I have my life because I love the light of the sky so unwoven with me.[3]

This is the poetry of hazy romance, not very high and yet the refined emotion leans on a half-divine mystic world of light and love. Sri Aurobindo goes deeper into the secret and presents it plainly and easily despite the problems of objective correlative. The style is different with its strong note of

---

2. Sri Aurobindo, *SABCL*, vol. 20, *The Synthesis of Yoga*, Sri Aurobindo Ashram, Pondicherry, p. 148.
3. Sisir Kumar Das ed., vol. I, p. 178.

masculinity, a bare grandeur and glory of the high spiritual peaks.

My mind beholds its veiled subconscient base,
All the dead obstinate symbols of the past,
The hereditary moulds, the stamps of race
Are upheld to sight, the old imprints effaced.

In a downpour of supernal light it reads
The black Inconscient's enigmatic script —
Recorded in a hundred shadowy screeds
An inert world's obscure enormous drift.[4]

This is the poetry of direct sight, the poetry of a deeper realization, a new kind of experience, which is presented in the form of subjective poetry. Tagore only prepares the path for such lyrics. Sri Aurobindo lacks the sweetness of Tagore or he has sacrificed sweetness in favour of great realizations and discoveries. Tagore is glad to feel the mysteries of Nature; Sri Aurobindo wishes to explore them.

The greatness of Tagore lies in his discovery of a music, which helps us perceive the message of Sri Aurobindo in the exact light. Tagore makes it easy for even the weakest soul to perceive the glory hidden behind the ordinary objects of Nature. This music opens the psychic being, our true self, and is able to build the basic foundation of Sri Aurobindo's *yoga*. His songs are often leading us to an integral realization, when we feel united with the whole universe.

Thou Hast made me known to friends whom I knew not. Thou hast given me seats in homes not my own. Thou hast brought the distant near and made a brother of the stranger. . . . Through birth and death, in this world or in others, wherever thou leadest me it is thou, the same, the one

4. Sri Aurobindo, *SABCL*, vol. 5, *Collected Poems*, p. 153.

> companion of my endless life who ever linkest my heart with bonds of joy to the unfamiliar.
>
> When one knows thee, then alien there is none, then no door is shut. Oh, grant me my prayer that I may never lose the bliss of the touch of the one in the play of the many.[5]

This is the *yoga* of integral realization expressed in terms of poetry. Time and again, Sri Aurobindo's wonderful expository prose harps on the same note. He seeks to clarify the ways of achieving this realization.

> There is one fundamental perception indispensable towards any integral knowledge or many-sided experience of this Infinite. It is to realize the Divine in its essential self and truth unaltered by forms and phenomena. Otherwise we are likely to remain caught in the net of appearances or wander confusedly in a chaotic multitude of cosmic or particular aspects, and if we avoid this confusion, it will be at the price of getting chained to some mental formula or shut up in a limited personal experience. The one secure and all reconciling truth which is the very foundation of the universe is this that life is the manifestation of an uncreated Self and Spirit and the key to life's hidden secret is the true relation of this Spirit with its own created existences. There is behind all this life the look of an eternal Being upon its multitudinous becoming. . . .[6]

Sri Aurobindo is talking here of the possibilities of every individual. The ultimate aim, both for Tagore and Sri Aurobindo, is to create an ideal society. As society is the enlargement of the individual, both of them seek to explore the possibilities of creating better individuals. The abolition

---

5. Sisir Kumar Das ed., vol. I, p. 64.
6. Sri Aurobindo, *SABCL*, vol. 20, p. 106.

of ego and the birth of love ensure the expansion of the human consciousness.

> Our spirit finds its larger self in the whole world, and is filled with an absolute certainty that is immortal. It dies a hundred times in its enclosures of self; for separateness is doomed to die, it cannot be made eternal. But it never can die where it is one with the All, for there is its truth, its joy.[7]

The only way to change the earth is to change the consciousness of the individual. The transformation of earth can come only by the expansion of the self and the sublimation of the ego. Both of them know well about the method: love. Sri Aurobindo observes in *The Human Cycle*:

> A spiritualized society would live like its spiritual individuals, not in the ego, but in the spirit, not as the collective ego, but as the collective soul. This freedom from the egoistic standpoint would be its first and most prominent characteristic.[8]

But, every individual has to be free and should be allowed to be unique. This variety will enrich society. It will be a kind of diversified oneness. Each man has to grow into the Divine within himself through his own individual being. The two are poets in love with this earth. Therefore, the beauty of the Light must descend on earth to give it a new look.

---

7. Sisir Kumar Das ed., vol. II, p. 324.
8. Sri Aurobindo, *SABCL,* vol. 15, *Social Writings,* pp. 239-40.

Books for Further Reading

Ayyub, Abu Sayeed, *Modernism and Tagore*, tr. by Amitava Ray, New Delhi: Sahitya Akademi, 1995.

Bhattacharya, Murari M., *Man: A Multiple Personality*, Pondicherry: Sri Aurobindo Society, 1985.

Bose, Buddhadeva, *Tagore : Portrait of a Poet*, Calcutta: Papyrus, 1994.

Bose, Nemai Sadhan, Foreword in *Rabindranath Tagore in Perspective : A Bunch of Essays*, Kolkata: Visva Bharati, 1989.

Chakrabarti, Ajitkumar, *Kavyaparikroma*, Calcutta: Visva Bharati, 1997.

Chunkapura, Jose, *The God of Rabindranath Tagore*, Kolkata: Visva Bharati, 2002.

Das, Manoj, *Sri Aurobindo in the First Decade of the Twentieth Century*, Pondicherry: Sri Aurobindo Ashram, 2003.

Deshpande, R.Y. (ed.), *Perspectives of Savitri*, vol. I and vol. II, Pondicherry: Aurobharati Trust, 2000 and 2002.

Deshpande, R.Y., *Sri Aurobindo and the New Millennium*, Pondicherry: Aurobharati Trust, 1999.

Dyson, Ketaki Kushari, *In Your Blossoming Flower-Garden: Rabindranath Tagore and Victoria Ocampo*, New Delhi: Sahitya Akademi, 1996.

Ghosal, Goutam, *Sri Aurobindo and World Literature*, Pondicherry: Sri Mira Trust, 2000.

Ghose, Sankho, *E Aamir Aaboron*, Kolkata: Papyrus, 1998.

Ghose, Sisirkumar, (ed.), *Angel of Surplus: Some Essays and Addresses on Aesthetics*: Rabindranath Tagore, Calcutta: Visva Bharati, 1978.

Ghose, Sisirkumar, *Rabindranath Tagore*, New Delhi: Sahitya Akademi, 1986.

Ghose, Sisirkumar, *The Poetry of Sri Aurobindo*, Chatuskone Private Limited, 1969.

Gokak, V.K., *Sri Aurobindo: Seer and Poet*, New Delhi: Abhinav Publications, 1973.

Gupta, Nolini Kanta, *Collected Works of Nolini Kanta Gupta, Essays on Mysticism*, vol. 2, Pondicherry: Sri Aurobindo International Centre of Education, 1971.

Iyengar, K.R.S., *Indian Writing in English,* Bombay: Asia Publishing House, 1962.

Kripalini, Krishna, *Rabindranath Tagore : A Life*, New Delhi: National Book Trust, 1985.

Lal, P., ed., *Modern Indian Poetry in English,* Calcutta: Writers Workshop, 1969.

Mcdermott, Robert A. (ed.), *Six Pillars: Introduction to the Major Works of Sri Aurobindo*, USA: Wilson Books, Pennsylvania, 1974.

Naik, M.K., *Aspects of Indian Writing in English : Essays in Honour of Professor K.R. Srinivasa Iyengar*, Delhi: Macmillan, 1979.

Nandakumar, Prema, *Dante and Sri Aurobindo: A Comparative Study : "The Divine Comedy" and "Savitri,"* New Delhi: Affiliated East-West Press Pvt. Ltd., 1981.

Price, Joan, *An Introduction to Sri Aurobindo's Philosophy*, Pondicherry: Sri Aurobindo Ashram, 2001.

Radhakrishnan, S. and a team of editors, *Rabindranath Tagore* : A Centenary Volume, 1861-1961, New Delhi: Sahitya Akademi, 1961.

Radice, William (trs.), *Rabindranath Tagore : Selected Poems*, New Delhi: Penguin Books, 1985.

Radice, William (trs.), *Rabindranath Tagore: Selected Short Stories*, New Delhi: Penguin Books, 2000.

Roarke, Jesse, *Sri Aurobindo*, Pondicherry: Sri Aurobindo Ashram, 1973.

Sethna, K. D. (Intro.), in *The English Language and the Indian Spirit: Correspondence between Kathleen Raine and K.D. Sethna*, Pondicherry: Sri Aurobindo Ashram, 1986.

Sethna, K.D., *Sri Aurobindo: the Poet*, Pondicherry: Sri Aurobindo International Centre of Education, 1970.

Sri Aurobindo, *Sri Aurobindo Birth Centenary*, vols. 1-30, Pondicherry: Sri Aurobindo Ashram, 1972.

Srinivasa Iyengar, K.R., *Sri Aurobindo: A Biography and a History*, 4th rev. edn., Pondicherry: Sri Aurobindo Ashram, 1985.

Tagore, Rabindranath, *Rabindra Rachanaboli* in 18 Volumes, Calcutta: Visva-Bharati, 2005.

Tagore, Rabindranath, *The English Writings of Rabindranath Tagore*, New Delhi: Sahitya Akademi, vol. 1, 1994, vol. 2, 1996, vol. 3, 1996.

Thompson, Edward, *Rabindranath Tagore: Poet and Dramatist*, Calcutta: RDDHI-INDIA, with a new appendix added by Sankha Ghosh, 1979.

Walsh, William, *Readings in Commonwealth Literature*, Oxford: Clarendon, 1973.

Index